Positive Finance

A Toolkit for Responsible Transformation

"In just a small number of thoughtfully written pages, Guez and Zaouati capture one of the truly critical agendas in sustainable development of our time: how to make capital work in the best interests of society. As their conclusion says, the question that any financial institution calling itself responsible must address is not "how is it done?" but "what does it achieve?". This focus on outcomes, on impact, is a prerequisite for success in a world that has set itself ambitious 15-year goals to end poverty, insecurity and climate change; a world that sometimes feels on a collision course with the short-termist behaviour of financial markets. This book makes a compelling case for change. It points to the enormous opportunities implicit in responsible investment, not purely for the large institutional funds that will benefit from a flourishing green economy, but for the whole investment chain including, most importantly, the general public whose savings underpin financial markets. Read this book and be inspired—finance has taken centre-stage in the sustainability debate."

Dr Jake Reynolds, Director, Sustainable Economy, Cambridge Institute for Sustainability Leadership

"Hervé Guez and Philippe Zaouati get straight to the point: the market is unfair, shortsighted, exhibits irrational exuberance and is shepherded by sheep. There is a need for a new paradigm to enable Positive Finance. The capacity is there, the ideas are plenty: now, what we need is action. *Positive Finance* is a call for action to make sustainable growth a reality, to get out of the tyranny of the short term and embrace a long-term perspective. This is an engaging and provocative book. Clear, direct, and illustrated with rich examples, the book brings real insights and keys to build a Positive Finance. It challenges every one of us, financial actors, executives, students and citizens, to rethink finance as a set of tools in the service of a sustainable development. As Guez and Zaouati rightly say: this is not about revolutionizing finance; it is about changing our focus and thinking of finance as a solution. A vital shift for embracing Positive Finance."

Céline Louche, Associate Professor in Corporate Social Responsibility, Head of CSR Research Axis and Joint-Head of Microfinance Chair at Audencia School of Management

POSITIVE FINANCE

A TOOLKIT FOR RESPONSIBLE TRANSFORMATION

HERVE GUEZ
AND PHILIPPE ZAOUATI

FOREWORD BY JACQUES ATTALI

Routledge
Taylor & Francis Group

LONDON AND NEW YORK

First published 2016 by Greenleaf Publishing Limited

Published 2017 by Routledge
2 Park Square, Milton Park, Abingdon, Oxon OX14 4RN
711 Third Avenue, New York, NY 10017, USA

Routledge is an imprint of the Taylor & Francis Group, an informa business

Copyright © 2016 Taylor & Francis

Cover by Sadie Gornall-Jones

British Library Cataloguing in Publication Data:
A catalogue record for this book is available from the British Library.

ISBN-13: 978-1-78353-516-3 [hbk]
ISBN-13: 978-1-78353-455-5 [pbk]

Contents

Figures, tables and boxes

Figures

Table

Boxes

Foreword

Jacques Attali

The word "finance" comes from the Old French word *finer,* meaning to "bring to a successful conclusion": which, indeed, pretty much sums it up. We urgently need to move beyond the pendulum swings of crises and sanctions to encourage a circular economy capable of a genuinely sustainable recovery.

The positive economy is today at the same stage of development as capitalism at the beginning of the 18th century: namely, that of a movement with a promising foundation.

Like any civic initiative, this movement needs recognition, visibility, and energy. The approach adopted by Hervé Guez and Philippe Zaouati is valuable in part for providing these. As finance professionals and committed actors in the world of Responsible Investment, both authors have contributed to the process of reflection required to produce *Pour une économie positive* (*For a Positive Economy*), a task with which I was entrusted by the president of France.[1]

The present book expands on this process of reflection by providing a precise and lucid analysis of current and potential developments in positive finance. In particular, these pages describe the tremendous construction project that is innovative finance: to design new mechanisms for collaborative entrepreneurship serving the general good; labels to identify those financial instruments committed to positive investments; and ways of encouraging mass acceptance of these products among individual investors to promote social responsibility within financial markets. Among other accomplishments, the authors have designed a new index that reflects companies' social efforts and the environmental commitment of their economic models. The index is particularly geared toward smaller companies within the Large Cap spectrum. Guez and Zaouati employ this index in their professional lives, where it is part of the asset selection process for determining what companies their funds invest in, demonstrating that it is indeed possible to revive the original goal of finance: the efficient allocation of savings to meet the need for sustainable investments.

The limits of today's prevailing model are self-evident. The financial, economic, social, and moral crises we are undergoing can be attributed to the tyranny of short-term thinking. Irresponsible behavior and opacity in the markets have allowed finance to deviate from its course, shifting its channels away from the real economy. No recovery can be sustainable unless we address the long-term interests of the whole world, and take

---

1   *Pour une économie positive* (*For a Positive Economy*) (Paris: Éditions Fayard, 2013). This is a French government report by the special presidential commission empaneled under the chairmanship of Jacques Attali.

into account the generations to come when making our choices. Many initiatives are already under way, at companies and cooperatives or associations dedicated to microfinance, fair trade, and social entrepreneurship. These endeavors are already generating value, both social and financial. By showing how their guiding principles are applicable to finance, this work by Hervé Guez and Philippe Zaouati lays the cornerstone of a new finance. One of its principal merits, and a considerable one, is that it demonstrates how modern finance can reconnect with the economy—if both become positive.

1

Introduction

For some, finance is "the enemy," the sole culprit of our latest economic crisis, and the manifestation of an obsolete model that has placed us on a collision course with social and environmental calamity. Such a view is understandable. The consequences of an ongoing "financialization" of the economy are tightly bound to the financial system's meltdown in 2007 and 2008—especially the excessive risk-taking promoted by the banking sector's compensation model and a corresponding broadening of the income gap to new proportions. This reached a paroxysm with the sub-prime mortgage crisis, aka: how to burden your clients with crippling debt while assuming zero risk. Public authorities all over the world have responded to the problem with an unprecedented avalanche of regulatory measures. These have included: attempts (rapidly abandoned) to segregate banks' proprietary trading activities; increased treasury and liquidity requirements for financial institutions and similar regulations for insurance companies; and tighter regulation of the derivatives market and constraints on compensation. However, the effectiveness of these efforts is called into doubt by a number of factors, not least among them a well-mounted and vigorous defense on the part of the financial sector. This is reinforced by the fact that the excesses of the financial system are merely symptomatic of an outdated economic model. Finance professionals simply adhered to a time-honored economic dogma, behaving like perfect *Homo economicus.*

That said, what is to be done? Should we be trading in our current model for that of the "positive economy" and injecting a heavy dose of altruism into our mechanisms of exchange, as was suggested by the focus group chaired by French economist and author Jacques Attali, founding president of the European Bank for Reconstruction and Development and former presidential advisor?[1] Of course, absolutely! Such a course involves a profound shift that is both essential and hopeful in nature. And, while resistance to change remains strong, the urgency of our situation forbids us from yielding to such pressures. Yet there is perhaps another, more humble, way forward—a complementary rather than alternative path: treating the financial realm itself as a "toolkit" able to provide a solution to the crisis. After all, transforming the economic model and bridging the ever-widening chasm of inequality—while respecting environmental constraints—is likely to prove tremendously expensive. In order to support social and technological innovations, to build new, more sustainable infrastructure and to finance the energy transition, we need to rethink how capital is allocated. We need to deploy savings to satisfy the needs of a positive economy. Reimagined, finance could become a powerful instrument at the service of this transition.

Of course, thinking of finance as a solution, as a tool for building a positive economy, does involve a certain overhaul,

---

1   *Ibid.*

and, perhaps, a bit of renunciation. For one thing, *Homo economicus* will have to go, as will the notion that financial markets always arrive at a fair price. We will then have to adjust to the reality that finance must take into account the general good. Finance is by no means an "objective" tool; it can be positive, or positively harmful, depending on how it is employed. When we make use of a financial mechanism, we need to ask ourselves to what end we are doing so. Finance can no longer justify its existence by pointing to services of which it is the primary beneficiary. Getting back to basics, the *function* of financial operations ought and must be to aggregate capital and invest it: in other words, to direct capital towards companies or projects. One has to admit that the markets, especially stock markets, are doing a poor job of fulfilling this role. But, if capital should be collected, then from whom? Invested in what and to what end? It is no longer possible for us to delegate these crucial decisions to the market's invisible hand.

The new paradigm we propose is one in which finance is concerned with the general good, which it furthers by investing savings in projects that offer added social and environmental value. However, because it involves future generations, added value from these endeavors can only be defined and measured over the medium and long term. Finance must return to the long view so as to be in sync with our social and environmental concerns.

Just how are we to shift the horizon and make positive finance the cornerstone of a truly positive economy, rather than an errant chip off the block of capitalist activity or merely a form of whitewash? Let us be clear: a positive economy is *not* the same thing as the real economy, a term often thrown around, but frequently signifying little more than the pursuit of business as usual. Talking about the real economy is no solution by itself:

the economy will have to change in order to become sustainable and positive.

We invest in the world we create; the converse is also true. As a result, the way savings are handled plays a crucial role in the transformation of finance and of the economy. Let's look at why.

Since 2006, more than 1,300 financial institutions, asset managers, pension funds, institutional investors, consultants, and ratings agencies have signed the United Nations "Principles for Responsible Investment" (PRI). In doing so, they have committed to investing in structures and projects that respect the environment, social issues, and rules of good governance. Among them, these 1,300 or so entities manage very considerable sums; if they were to genuinely respect their engagements, their collective strength would be enormous. But, despite very encouraging numbers,[2] Socially Responsible Investing (SRI) remains a niche market at the periphery of the financial world, like an exception that serves to confirm the general rule. Actors in the world of finance alternate between extreme caution, often the watchword of large investors, who are risk-averse, and more adventurous approaches, which are confined to specialized units with limited impact. This explains to a great extent why SRI has often been dismissed as *greenwashing.*

---

2   According to Novethic, a subsidiary of the Caisse des Dépôts et Consignations, which has been observing the SRI market in France for a decade, the assets under management of SRI funds have risen from €3.9 billion to €169.7 billion over the 2003–2013 period, increasing 40 times over in 10 years. See "2013 Figures on Responsible Investment in France: Novethic's 10th Market Survey," www.novethic.fr/fileadmin/user_upload/tx_ausy-novethicetudes/pdf_syntheses/French_RI_market_2013.pdf, accessed September 19, 2015.

The general apathy toward Responsible Investment is partially due to incomprehension on the part of the public from whom savings are drawn. SRI is too sketchy a concept for the moment. What is all this *for*, individual investors ask? How can one even measure the social or environmental impact of this kind of investment? Does SRI actually influence the actions and behavior of corporations? To answer these questions, a group of French asset management professionals ventured to formulate a concise definition in 2013. Aimed at the wider public, this definition does something new by emphasizing the goals of SRI, focusing on "why" instead of "how." The definition thus explains that SRI funds invest in "companies which contribute to sustainable development." That sounds perfectly straightforward; however, practically speaking, what does it mean? There are several ways in which companies can contribute to sustainable development. They can mitigate their social and environmental risks by addressing the general interest through robust Corporate Social Responsibility (CSR); however, they can also offer innovations, develop energy-saving products and create new services that improve the world we live in.

Thus, a responsible investor is attentive to the quality of CSR policies and committed to being a responsible shareholder: for instance, by voting at general meetings and engaging in dialogue with company management. But such investors need to be granted more power. Management of publicly traded corporations is controlled by shareholders according to complex mechanisms designed to align the interests of these two groups. This arrangement has a marked tendency to promote a focus on shareholder return, if necessary at the expense of any and all social or environmental concerns. It is high time we restored the executive role of caring for the corporation as such, which means all of its many stakeholders: its shareholders certainly, but also its employees, clients, creditors, and its environment. How can this be done? In part by restructuring shareholders' rights to accord greater weight, in terms of dividends and voting rights, to shareholders who maintain their presence for an extended period, who are thus genuinely implicated in the company's strategic planning and who are therefore responsible investors.

Influencing corporate behavior through enhanced CSR or by financing innovative technologies certainly contributes to shaping a more positive economy. However, the issues we face call for even bolder measures. Savings can create and support new models, such as green growth, or the third industrial revolution, that are founded on rational altruism and sharing.[3]

First of all, the ecological transition: how can we finance energy-efficient residential renovation on a large scale—especially when occupants lack the resources to invest in onerous building work? How do we ensure that future energy savings cover the cost of investments made today? How can we accelerate the development of renewable energy in emerging countries? Traditional models of finance are not designed to address these questions. Risks need to be distributed differently among public authorities, private investors, users and technology providers. A new form of partnership between the public and private is needed. A similar overhaul is required in order to enable the financing of alternative production models, particularly that known as the "circular economy." Granted, finance is showing

---

3   This concept is well described by the American essayist Jeremy Rifkin, in *The Third Industrial Revolution: How Lateral Power is Transforming Energy, the Economy, and the World*. (London: Palgrave Macmillan, 2011).

a growing interest in green growth, particularly when it comes to financing renewable energy, which is currently heavily subsidized in a considerable number of countries. This enthusiasm, however, does not by any means signify that the energy transition as an issue has been resolved. Creating or renovating infrastructure for the production and transport of energy, improving the energy efficiency of our buildings and lifestyle, and preparing for climate change are all projects demanding enormous investments that involve complex risks: not least because any results are far in the future and heavily contingent on future developments in technology. Financing such a vast transformation takes both determination and genuine innovation.

The topic of financing has been raised in Europe, where it has taken the form of a "2020 Climate and Energy Package."[4] At the global level, the issue is currently being treated in the context of the OECD and G20, with a proliferation of initiatives aimed at directing savings toward financing the energy transition and, indeed, "positive" infrastructure more generally. This new trend could radically accelerate the process, giving rise to a wide market in financing for the energy transition. Here, money could be "earmarked,"[5] transparently permitting investors to allocate their resources based on informed choices. Though still in its infancy, a striking illustration of this type of solution is the

---

4   See ec.europa.eu/clima/policies/strategies/2020/index_en.htm, accessed June 12, 2015. At a national level, France produced a "Feuille de route pour la transition écologique," which was presented in late 2012. The topic of financing returned to the spotlight in November 2013, following the government's publication of a *Livre blanc sur le financement de la transition* écologique, and the banking and finance conference held in 2014.

5   "Earmarked" is here used in its literal sense of tracking, to make sure we know how money invested is actually spent.

green bond market, which consists of products destined to finance environmentally responsible infrastructure that bring together private investors and public authorities.

Similar financial innovations can also be placed in the service of social objectives. The concatenation of demographic and economic pressures has exacerbated inequalities at every level of our societies, leaving traditional financial models ill equipped to address the needs of society's poorest members. It is practically impossible to stir interest in projects or services that appear unprofitable, or too small, or geared toward what is often called "the bottom of the pyramid." Ever since the success of the Grameen Bank and the Nobel Prize awarded to its founder, Muhammad Yunus, microfinance has been a recognized and respected activity which has demonstrated how poverty can be reduced on a significant scale, entirely thanks to financial innovation. Microfinance has experienced its share of difficulties in its growth process but, more importantly, it finances only a marginal portion of economic activity. Can its core model be generalized? Are there other financial innovations we could imagine that can help to reconcile adequate returns on savings and solutions to pervasive social problems? This is the central question for impact investing—and attempts are under way to find answers. In 2013, the British presidency of the G8 decided to place social impact investment on the agenda to illustrate that the United Kingdom's Liberal-led government was ahead of the curve in this area. It is certainly true that the country has innovated considerably in the realm of social sector financing— including the creation of a major public fund for financing social initiatives[6] and the launch of Social Impact Bonds (SIB)—very

6   "Big Society Capital" was created in 2012 by the UK government as a means of financing social enterprise. Two-thirds of its €700 million in

probably because the state is withdrawing from this domain. Rising sovereign debt in all developed nations is pushing authorities to disengage from a number of costly social programs, even as widening inequalities are forcing a larger segment of the population toward the margins of societies.

In its present form, the notion that investment can produce a "social return" (SROI) is new, and gives rise to financing mechanisms lying at the intersection of public, non-profit, and private enterprise that combine many of the functional aspects formerly specific to each of these sectors. These innovative instruments, commonly grouped under the term "impact investing," are situated halfway between socially responsible investing (which continues to privilege financial return) and philanthropy (for which financial return is considered irrelevant). In France, this forms what is called the *économie sociale et solidaire* (the social and solidarity economy), and constitutes a non-negligible 10% of the country's jobs. From May 2012 to March of 2014, this sector even had its own ministry, and its development is a topic at the European level as well, thanks to initiatives by former European Commissioner Michel Barnier and the creation of a fund for social entrepreneurship. But, although the tools are in place, social finance remains marginal: all too often entrenched in defensive militant positions, and thus unable to adapt to innovations or the emergence of a new type of social entrepreneur. Nonetheless, new approaches that are less fearful of finance continue to appear. Social Impact Bonds (SIBs) are one archetypal example.

capital will be provided by transfers from dormant accounts at British banks. See Mark King, "Dormant accounts to fund 'big society' bank," *The Guardian*, July 19, 2010; www.theguardian.com/money/2010/jul/19/dormant-accounts-fund-big-society-bank, accessed August 2, 2015.

The aim of these securities is to finance social programs using private funds (rehabilitation, reintegration, recidivism prevention, social housing, care for the homeless, etc.). Investor compensation is a function of each project's success, creating a new generation of Public–Private Partnerships (PPPs). However, this new business model is open to question on several fronts. To begin with, is it not dangerous to "privatize" certain types of social services? But, as pointed out by the United Kingdom's prime minister David Cameron, there are some things that the government does not do well: areas where other agents, such as social enterprises, charities, and voluntary bodies, may perform better.[7] The topic is inexhaustible.

In any event, it is clear that, in order to accelerate the ecological transition and resolve social challenges, whether in developed or developing countries, the intelligent mobilization of capital is crucial. Equally important is the serious upstream analysis of projects from a financial and extra-financial standpoint, the measurement of investments' impact, and a reconciliation of finance with the general good. Achieving these transformations, which are closely tied to a new vision of how to allocate savings, demands greater transparency, clear definitions for concepts, recognized labels and the smart deployment of public funds to provide incentives for private actors.

---

7   D. Cameron, "Social enterprises, charities and voluntary bodies have the knowledge, human touch and personal commitment to succeed where governments often fail," speech presented at the Social Impact Investment Forum, London, UK, June 6, 2013; https://www.gov.uk/government/speeches/prime-ministers-speech-at-the-social-impact-investment-conference, accessed September 19, 2015.

2

Positive Finance for a positive economy

Before turning to the role of finance, we need to make a small detour via economics and, even further afield, to geology. What kind of a world do we live in today? What makes us so sure that the changes we currently face are not merely the result of traditional microeconomic or macroeconomic cycles? Why are our economic models, which have weathered several centuries in some cases, now obsolete? In 2002, the Nobel prizewinning geochemist Paul Crutzen claimed that the Earth entered a new geological era two centuries ago, an age characterized by the capacity of humankind to radically alter the environment. In the course of what he has dubbed the "Anthropocene" era, which opened with the Industrial Revolution, it is expected that the world's human population will grow exponentially until finally stabilizing, around the year 2050, at close to nine billion inhabitants.

The demographic explosion has occurred alongside an even faster increase in the total goods produced by humankind. This unprecedented growth has led us to consume natural resources without concern for how they are to be renewed, and to destroy tremendous numbers of living species. It also has a strong impact on natural cycles such as those of nitrogen, carbon, and other greenhouse gases, now commonly referred to as GHGs, which contribute to rising temperatures and affect the planet's climate. Our ecological footprint, a sort of environmental accounting system that emerged from the Rio Summit in 1992, indicates that we currently use more than 1.5 times the carrying capacity of our planet.

FIGURE 1: **How history was made: a century-by-century breakdown of human life and wealth alongside atmospheric carbon levels**

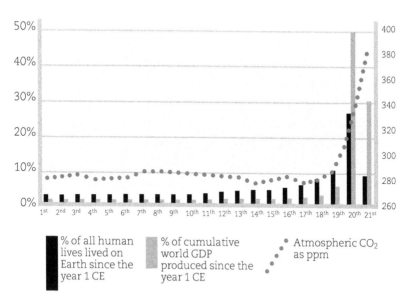

Homo Economicus is ill adapted to survival in the Anthropocene

Such radical changes to the global ecosystem will inevitably have repercussions for the functioning of human economies. First among these is the extinction of the species known as *Homo economicus*, theorized by the 19th-century Italian economist Vilfredo Pareto.[1]

Roughly speaking, this concept describes humans as calculating beings that seek at all times to maximize their individual self-interest. Among other things, it makes economics an exact science: the art of best allocating limited resources to satisfy potentially unlimited wants. However, as several centuries of economic theory can attest, the conceptual basis that underpins *Homo economicus* is unsound, because it is entirely too simplistic. Human beings are an inextricable combination of reason *and* emotion, sometimes egotistical, sometimes altruistic, and motivated by aspirations too complex and contradictory to be contained within a single rational framework. Happiness is not a linear function modeling the satisfaction of material needs . . . But who cares, some economists would say, as long as the model runs more or less smoothly?

However, to say that *Homo economicus* "runs" is a terrific understatement, looking at the exponential economic growth we have observed since the appearance of the species. Unfortunately, this frenetic drive to meet created needs that are ceaselessly reinvented is exhausting; it provides ever-dwindling levels of satisfaction while devastating the resources on which

---

1   Alexander Brink (ed.), *Corporate Governance and Business Ethics* (Dordrecht, The Netherlands and New York: Springer Science and Business Media, 2011), p. ix.

our lives depend at an unprecedented rate. *Homo economicus* is a performative concept—the theory shapes reality. By imagining the economy as a world peopled with perfectly rational agents, entirely motivated by the pursuit of personal interest, we have brought into being a society that reflects this vision of the world. Such a society induces anxiety because dissatisfaction is endemic and ubiquitous. It also gives rise to ever-increasing individualism, at the risk of jeopardizing the necessary bonds of a social contract, and at the expense of all concern for the general good and well-being of future generations. The rising incidence of psychosocial disorders in wealthy societies, like the dearth of efforts implemented so far to fend off the consequences of climate change, is a disturbing symptom. The *business as usual* scenario does not appear to envisage alternate outcomes to massive burnout or a general and definitive *game over*.

Our so-called rational actor, *Homo economicus,* rationally belongs to an outdated vision of humanity. We have entered a new era, one in need of new models and ways of thinking accompanied by new tools for allocating capital and governing an economy that will, out of necessity, become zero-emission and circular. Clearly, we are on the brink of a long transitional period, full of questions and dilemmas, challenges and innovations.

Things have to change, but how? Must we wait until a new local, national, and global order becomes obvious to all, with a new framework, new objectives and the capacity to bring these to fruition? Or, on the contrary, should everyone, each in their own spheres of activity, set about inventing tools and practices that are more respectful of the general interest? To take the case of finance: how do we ensure that regulations issued by public authorities and private initiatives are intelligently coordinated?

Before we even begin answering the question of *how*, such actions need to be situated within a coherent discourse, a narrative of sorts.

A number of authors have contributed to drafting the shape of a revised model for economic development, which we might schematically describe as follows:

- The function of an economy is not the accumulation of wealth but the search for well-being and personal fulfillment. This is beautifully described by Amartya Sen, the Indian economist and Nobel laureate, through the concept of "capability."[2]. This refers to an individual's available freedom to choose the type of life he or she would like to live. Clearly, it is capability that we must seek to maximize, rather than wealth. Of course, the two often go together but only up to a certain point, and the extent of such well-being depends more on the difference between one's income and the norm than any calculable degree of opulence.

- Our search for well-being must henceforth incorporate environmental concerns if we are to guarantee the future of civilization, possibly even the human species. As Hans Jonas points out in *The Imperative of Responsibility*,[3] concern for the environment has become pressing. The technologies we rely on today run the risk of depleting our limited natural resources. However—and this is the terrifying paradox—our well-being is largely tethered

---

2   Amartya Sen, *Commodities and Capabilities* (New York: Elsevier Science Pub., 1985).

3   Hans Jonas, *The Imperative of Responsibility: In Search of Ethics for the Technological Age* (Chicago: University of Chicago Press, 1984).

to these technologies, which transform these precious natural resources into energy and goods.

- The quest to further the general good is not an option, but an obligation. Decisions made by our theoretical *Homo economicus* do not naturally lead to our reaching social and environmental goals that have now become paramount. Therefore, we need regulations or voluntary practices that encourage real, ordinary *Homo sapiens,* who are not always rational, to behave altruistically as a means of preserving the long-term general interest. The concept of Corporate Social Responsibility is a legitimate notion, and ought to first and foremost address questions of sustainable development. It is therefore logical that national and international regulations in this area be multiplied.

- Finally, citizens, the actual consumers who spend and save, must have opportunities to voice their social and environmental concerns through their purchases and investments. Disclosure is crucial to making this possible.

This anticipated shift toward a sustainable future will also intimately involve one of the economy's major mechanisms, particularly reviled in recent years: namely, the financial markets.

Before moving on to the chapters dedicated to innovation, which we hope will be encouraging, let us first take a brief look at the picture of what needs to change.

The financial markets need to grow up

The global 2008 crisis and its aftermath engendered a general indictment of finance, which was accused of opacity, complexity, cronyism and unwarranted protections, excessive risk-taking, and unjustified compensation practices. Rather than the whole of the financial sector, the blame has been laid primarily on the recent functioning of the financial markets. However, criticizing the workings of the financial markets calls into question much more than the business of finance. Indeed, banks, asset management companies, and hedge funds are far from the only players in these markets. Companies and states increasingly fulfill their capital requirements on these same markets. Insurance companies and pension funds, both public and private, invest the greater part of their reserves and excess cash. Individuals do much the same with a significant portion of their savings, particularly in the form of mutual funds and other pooled investment vehicles. The problem is not so much the "financialization" of the economy, as the pervasive role of the "market" in every aspect of economic life. To put it differently, this critique concerns not only the financial sector, but all economic agents.

To confront these challenges, there are two ideological pitfalls to avoid. On the one hand is a desire to simply do without financial markets altogether or "put them in their place." In practice, this means putting them under government control and adopting a form of state capitalism. On the other hand, to take the opposite view, the dysfunctions observed are merely temporary turbulence, and support further liberalization to improve the efficiency of the financial markets. Nor is the middle road (which we often see adopted) the best solution; it has created an accelerated form of "re-regulation." Following a period of undoubtedly reckless deregulation, this impulse seems legitimate, desirable even. However, this path risks missing the heart of the matter and possibly even being counterproductive, because it takes a tempting shortcut according to which a crisis equates to a call for risk reduction. However, risk and risk-taking are essential drivers of both innovation and investment: drivers we need more than ever to finance the ecological transition and promote an economy based on well-being. The crux of the problem is not so much risk-taking as it is the very notion of risk as it is commonly applied to the financial markets.

A very timely and acute analysis of the British financial markets was conducted in 2012 by economist John Kay at the behest of the UK government's Secretary of State for Business, Innovation and Skills.[4] *The Kay Review,* as it is known, found the models used to calculate pricing and the metrics employed to gauge risk prevailing in the markets to be significant impediments to the creation of "positive markets" that can offer solutions to the long-term challenges facing our societies. In other words, these models prevent the financial markets from fulfilling their social function, which is to efficiently allocate capital within the economy. Likewise, asset management models based on Modern Portfolio Theory—which is modern in name only—lead to prices that are in no way "fair," since they are based on

---

4   J. Kay, *The Kay Review of UK Equity Markets and Long-Term Decision-Making: Final Report,* UK Department for Business Innovation and Skills, July 2012; webarchive.nationalarchives.gov.uk/20121204121011/ http://www.bis.gov.uk/assets/biscore/business-law/docs/k/12-917-kay-review-of-equity-markets-final-report.pdf, accessed October 22, 2015. Modern Portfolio Theory (MPT) was developed in 1952 by Harry Markowitz. Its fundamental tenet is that it is in the best interests of a rational investor to diversify investments in order to maximize returns at the least possible risk.

mathematical calculations derived from assumptions that are, by definition, incomplete.

In the book *Illusion financière* (*The Financial Illusion*),[5] French mathematical economist Gaël Giraud explains that relying on financial markets to price securities simply cannot achieve a satisfactory balance. There are basically four reasons for this. The first two are structural in nature and should be enough to make us definitively give up on the whole idea of a "fair" or "equilibrium" price: namely, the perverse influence of crowd effects and our systematic cognitive bias in favor of the present. The remaining two explanations are more circumstantial: the development and standardization of index-based (passive) asset management on the one hand, and the broad disregard for social utility in the investment decision-making process. These latter tendencies are more likely to respond to improved regulation or practices than the first two.

The financial markets are not "fair"

So what are the assumptions of the aforementioned mathematical models for calculating price and risk exposure? In short, they claim that markets are *efficient*. According to this fable, if all the *Homo economicus* were to get together in one place, these assets would be assessed at their "fair" price. The underlying idea is not illogical—any economic actor seeking to sell an asset attempts to rationally calculate its worth.[6] Such an agent will make predictions forecasting changes in micro- and macroeconomic environment, conduct market research if a corporate entity, and try to anticipate inflation trends. Since our agent is

---

5   Gaël Giraud, *Illusion financière* (Paris: Éditions de l'Atelier, 2012).
6   The theoretical value of an asset is generally considered to be the net present value of all future revenue the asset will produce.

attempting to maximize self-interest, said agent will make every attempt to sell the asset at a price greater than that at which it is valued, or, conversely, to purchase an asset below this price. A market offers the useful feature of confronting the greatest possible number of buyers and sellers for any particular asset, such that transactions take place at a fair price, at the equilibrium point of all contending forces. Unfortunately, this theory fails to hold up in practice.

Markets exhibit irrational exuberance

To begin with, we can all together be altogether wrong: that is, be too optimistic or pessimistic in our projections of the market's growth, as has historically been the case for sugar, Internet startups, solar energy, and any number of other bubbles going back to the Dutch tulip. These collective errors are self-propagating and produce waves of panic or euphoria that are increasingly being studied by scientists in various disciplines. Bubbles and their bursting are thus indeed the products of this "irrational exuberance of the financial markets," to quote the famous expression coined, in a flash of extreme lucidity, by Alan Greenspan, former chairman of the US Federal Reserve.[7] Such exuberance is typical of crowd behavior.

Markets are shortsighted

Markets have a second failing resulting from their instantaneity, or, what is called in professional jargon, their "liquidity." Investors tend naturally to gravitate toward high-liquidity

---

7   From a speech given in 1996 at the American Enterprise Institute on the topic of the 1990s Internet bubble. In context, the expression was a warning to signify that overvaluation could be affecting equity markets.

markets because it is easier to find a buyer or seller at any given moment. Again, the underlying principle seems fairly sound. Pricing would clearly suffer if investors were routinely unable to quickly find a buyer for their securities, and investors would prefer to leave their money idle under the mattress rather than pour it into assets that contribute to the economy. Thus, liquidity is a necessary property of markets. The problem is that by seeking ever-greater liquidity we have undermined the foundations of the markets we rely on.

The behavior of economic actors also changes radically according to the liquidity of the assets they are investing in. Take an investor who is looking to buy an illiquid asset, such as a stake in an unlisted company, for instance. What is the most likely approach? Here, any rational actor would conduct an in-depth analysis to make sure that the asset is sound and the dividends it is expected to produce will materialize. Naturally, some expectation that the market value of these shares will rise enters into the equation; however, this resale value can only be envisaged for the medium term, and will not have a direct bearing on acquisition, but rather be the fortuitous consequence of a sensible investment.

The situation is quite different when the asset under consideration is very liquid and prices are adjusted every microsecond by an electronic marketplace. Here, hope of a quick profit becomes the overriding motivation for purchase in most cases. In hyperliquid markets, investors are most sensitive to factors likely to induce short-term variations in price, at the expense of those whose effects appear in the medium term. More concerning is that participants in these markets are no longer interested in an asset's fair value so much as the reactions of other players in the market. Whether the reaction is justified or merely the result of copycat behavior makes no difference. Who cares?! This derails the whole mechanism by which pricing is conducted. Far from being an encounter among rational actors acting on their opinion of the fundamental value of assets, the market is in fact populated by players who buy or sell according to an idea of how their fellows will, rightly or wrongly, behave.

Liquidity itself is not inherently good or bad. To some extent, it can contribute to better pricing but, when pushed to extremes, liquidity causes more harm than good. All things considered, short-term speculative transactions are less socially and economically useful than medium-term investments. We must therefore find mechanisms of some sort, whether fiscal or regulatory, which encourage the most beneficial forms of market participation. The rise of high-frequency trading hardly suggests we are currently on the right path.[8]

8   According to data from the New York Stock Exchange, the average hold time for a stock dropped from seven years in 1940 to less than six months in 2014—and some calculations put the average at an even more shocking 22 seconds! See Paul Farrow, "How long does the average share holding last? Just 22 seconds," *The Telegraph*, January 18, 2012; www.telegraph.co.uk/finance/personalfinance/investing/9021946/How-long-does-the-average-share-holding-last-Just-22-seconds.html; Robert C. Pozen, "Curbing Short-Termism in Corporate America: Focus on Executive Compensation," Brookings Institution, May 2014; www.brookings.edu/~/media/research/files/papers/2014/05/06-pozen/brookings_shorttermismfinal_may2014.pdf; and Sy Harding, "Stock market becomes short attention span theater of trading," *Forbes*, January 21, 2011 www.forbes.com/sites/greatspeculations/2011/01/21/stock-market-becomes-short-attention-span-theater-of-trading, all accessed July 26, 2015.

Markets are shepherded by the sheep

Another impediment to the smooth functioning of markets lies in the proliferation of passive or quasi-passive participants: that is to say, investors who are content to blindly allocate their cash reserves in accordance with market indices. They purchase securities without ever "in all good conscience" choosing one stock over another or preferring one sector to another. What logic motivates these investors, who make a point of having no opinion? One explanation is that they believe markets are actually efficient, such that the prices of all securities are, at any given moment, "fair" and it is consequently pointless to position oneself differently from anyone else, especially when short-term effects are hard to anticipate. Or, they are convinced that markets are not, in fact, efficient. Since it is then practically impossible to predict which managers or management styles are likely to produce reliably better results than the market as a whole, it is better to aim for the average, rather than to risk underperforming.

In the last few decades, investment fund managers have, for the most part attempted to duplicate, or at least stick close to the composition of a market-representative index such as the S&P 500, the CAC 40 and so on. Such funds are commonly known as index funds, tracker funds or, when the practice occurs in allegedly actively managed funds, index-huggers.[9] Investment decisions, rather than being guided by fundamental analysis (to the effect of, "I believe in the long-term growth of

---

9   Benchmarks are reference indices that serve as a point of comparison in measuring the performance of asset managers. Index-based management, also known as "passive management," involves strictly purchasing securities in the proportions exhibited by a particular stock market index. Benchmarked management, on the other hand, simply has guidelines to avoid straying too far from the composition of its reference.

this corporation"), are dictated by the relative weight of this or that security (stock or bond) in whatever reference index is used. Once again, the equilibrium of the pricing equation is nullified by participants who fail to allocate capital where they believe it will produce the best return, instead simply depositing it where it already is, since the companies dominating such indices are already enormous. For these investors, risk is defined as departing from the market average, as represented by the benchmark index; attempting to do better is prescribed as too dangerous, as though it were better to follow the herd wherever it might lead, even should this be over a cliff. Such behavior might be construed as rational if it could be limited to a single individual, but generalized it is dangerous, Similarly, a single rational individual might justify refusing vaccination as too risky or costly in a country where 99% of the population is vaccinated, but, widely practiced, this would have catastrophic effects on public health (and is generally prohibited by governments).

Markets are blind

If investors appear blinkered in the way they swear by indices, markets themselves are systematically blind to every aspect of a corporation that is not strictly speaking financial. By and large, Corporate Social Responsibility (CSR) is ignored in pricing models and investment decisions. This can be the result of either an ideological position, as in: "The social responsibility of business is to make money,"[10] or mere unwillingness to challenge convention. In fact, CSR is still rarely taught to students specializing in finance. Additionally, there are genuine practical and

---

10   Milton Friedman, "The Social Responsibility of Business is to Increase Profits," *The New York Times Magazine*, September 13, 1970.

technical obstacles to integrating the ethics of a corporation into attempts at valuation, as ethical criteria may not offer clear and consistent links with the financial value of a company. Regardless of why, the fact remains that, most of the time, the pricing of an asset fails to take into account human rights abuses or deleterious environmental consequences, be they acute or diffuse, unless they give rise to sanctions or subsidies.

For the financial markets, the utility of a project or company begins and ends with its capacity to produce monetary wealth. Without denying that the primary virtue of money is, after all, to render fungible assets that are not originally equivalent, it is absurd to take this to the extreme of believing that anything at all can be "monetized," and that everything of value has a price. The financial markets have today become cynical, and to borrow Oscar Wilde's famous quip, they "know the price of everything and the value of nothing!"[11]

A new paradigm to enable positive financial markets

But real-world financial markets are not, in fact, populated by *Homo economicus* of the perfectly rational and predictable variety, but quite simply of *Homo sapiens*, with their attendant strengths and weaknesses. These all-too-human beings of flesh and blood may collectively adopt the exuberant or compulsive behaviors of a gambling addict, or the docile placidity of sheep seeking the reassuring companionship of the flock. Within the crowd there will also be market players who are reasonable and

11   Oscar Wilde, *Lady Windermere's Fan,* 1892.

circumspect, making investment choices based on the fundamental value of each asset. Most of the time, market participants shift among these various behaviors. Knowing all this, can one really lend credence to the idea that the price of a security exposed to such a situation will miraculously be "fair?" One can, of course, affirm that "the market is always right" while observing that it changes its views daily. But then the postulate becomes posture, a dogma without basis in theory or fact.

Positive finance consists of reinjecting social and economic value into the functioning of markets. A number of investors already make decisions based on ethical, social, or environmental criteria. How can we encourage those actors who avoid reducing the utility of their investments to a mere matter of financial return? How can we establish practices or regulations conducive to behavior that promotes the general good? The regulations we need are not those currently being designed by most market authorities, which aim to limit risks. Instead, we require measures that can modify the way we conceive of risk itself, and thus how it is calculated. The attitude against which we must imperatively struggle is not the appetite for risk, but short-term thinking, blind conformism, and cynicism.

Long-term savings fit with long-term investments

We are facing a fundamental contradiction. The economy consists largely of long-term financing needs. Those with savings, however, would like their precautionary savings to be readily available, and thus have an overall preference for liquid markets. Putting aside the fable of an efficient market that would take care of reconciling all these opposing interests to a perfect outcome, any attempt at regulation must begin by acknowledging this contradiction, and on this basis:

- **Address the question of where to direct savings.** Precautionary savings do exist, but they hardly represent the bulk of household savings. Retirement savings, employee savings, and term life insurance policies are all designed to help ensure a prosperous future. Is it reasonable for such savings to be systematically channeled into the same vehicles as those "rainy day" savings? Could we not rather invent mechanisms that would direct the second type toward long-term investments, into investment projects offering, among other things, high social and environmental returns?

- **Establish mechanisms that encourage long-term savings directed toward investments of real use to the economy.**[12] We already have punitive measures for discouraging the most short-term transactions, such as high-frequency trading. This is the principle behind the tax on financial transactions known as the Tobin tax. Punitive systems are always a tempting option because they have an aura of simplicity. But such measures are in fact very difficult to implement in a world where production, including production of financial products, can easily be relocated. Although a positive approach can seem hard to apply at first (how does one go about defining what

12   For reasons of space and focus we do not address here a question that merits extensive treatment: how do we define and evaluate the social utility of a business or project? The question of social utility has given rise to a number of tentative definitions; however, none, as yet, appears fully satisfactory. Nonetheless, while no one is capable of precisely defining such utility, everyone knows it when they see it!

is *most* useful to the economy?) it has a better chance of succeeding in the long run. This is because, unlike production, a significant portion of savings cannot be exported.

Identifying *positive* savings vehicles

Naturally, positive finance cannot be reduced to the issue of savings. There are myriad subjects to consider, and one might do well to probe market mechanisms, the organization of the banking system, complex financial instruments, the potential of hedge funds to have costly impacts on markets, or the prevailing styles of pension fund management and sometimes unreasonable performance expectations they involve. However, the design of well-conceived savings vehicles constitutes a particularly powerful lever for addressing the problems described above. Redirecting savings toward "positive" products induces structural changes in the financial markets, and reaches out to us all, as savers and citizens.

So, how do we find and identify these positive savings products? Savings are predominately held by institutional investors (pension funds and insurers for the most part), or directly by individuals in the form of investment funds offered by banks (mutual funds, investment funds, etc.). Asset management companies play a key role in how these portfolios are managed, as they are the ones who create and manage investment funds, and to whom institutional investors delegate management via investment mandates. We need to draw on asset managers' capacity for innovation, and that of the financial industry as a whole. Financial engineering has already demonstrated its ability to invent all kinds of complex financial indicators for assessing the stability and growth of corporations, so we are entitled to consider it up to the task of designing useful indicators for evaluating companies on social and environmental matters. The most promising innovations are related to the most prominent approaches to responsible investing, namely:

- Investing the capital or debt of companies that meet not only economic performance criteria, but social and environmental ones as well. This is what is known as "Socially Responsible Investing" and commonly referred to as SRI;

- Financing projects that move the ecological transition forward;

- Impact investing.

These trends are real, but they are recent and consequently unstandardized. Yet, if we can avoid the pitfall of *greenwashing*, these innovative investment vehicles can be a strong driving force in the service of changing our economy.

3

Savings as a means of transforming the corporation

Savings—meaning the disposable income that is directly invested and funds located in the reserves of insurance companies or pension funds—serve largely to finance corporations via the equity and bond markets. Thus, it makes sense that savings be invested in enterprises concerned with their performance on a social, environmental, and economic level.

This type of focused, selective CSR-sensitive investment, commonly termed "Socially Responsible Investment," has taken shape over the last decade. Assets under management (AuM) have grown significantly and tools for analysis have been developed. A definition has also solidified: taking environmental, social, and governance (ESG) criteria into account alongside financial considerations. This conception of "responsible" is embodied concretely in the Principles for Responsible Investment (PRI), an initiative that grew out of the United Nations

Environment Programme's Finance Initiative (UNEP-FI) and was initially sponsored by a handful of large institutional investors. Since their launch in 2006, the PRI have met with nothing short of spectacular success. In fact, the organization's signatories represent 59 trillion US dollars, or 20% of the total volume represented by the world's capital markets![1]

FIGURE 2: **Progression of assets and number of signatories, UN-PRI**

Source: Mirova/UN-PRI

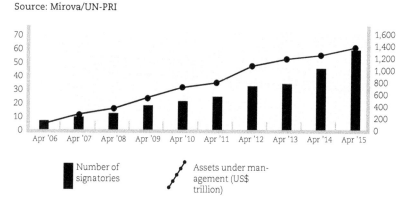

Given this tremendous financial power, how is it that we are not living in a fully renovated economy: well on its way to sustainable and harmonious development, combining respect for

---

1   For figures, see the UN-PRI website: www.unpri.org/news/pri-fact-sheet, accessed August 10, 2015, and Charles Roxburgh, Susan Lund, and John Piotrowski, "Mapping Global Capital Markets 2011," McKinsey & Co., August 2011; www.mckinsey.com/insights/global_capital_markets/mapping_global_capital_markets_2011, accessed August 10, 2015, for information on global capital markets.

human rights and greater well-being with control of climate risks and reasonable management of natural resources?

Getting back to the business of investing in the long term

Signatories of the PRI are committed to respecting six fundamental principles. First and foremost among these is the following: "We will incorporate ESG issues into investment analysis and decision-making processes." Now, if all of the PRI's signatories diligently applied this principle to the totality of their assets, Responsible Investing would indeed have 59 trillion dollars of assets under management! Of course, the slightest common sense observation dispatches this illusion; despite perfectly genuine growth of the Responsible Investment market, we are a long way from such numbers. But why?

There are two explanations we must get out of the way immediately; both are similarly naïve and equally simple, but nonetheless antithetical. The first is the more charitable: namely, that these commitments are not fully reflected in action because they are too recent, and signatories simply need more time to implement them. The second, significantly more cynical, consists in assuming that investors have signed on to the principles to improve their image, and have no sincere intention of taking action except in a cosmetic fashion.

Knowing these institutions as we do, the authors are convinced that the signatories are, for the most part, acting in good faith. If they are having trouble shifting from declaring their intentions to practical applications it is because they have trouble combining long-term objectives with the typically short-term management styles that are a legacy of outdated financial concepts. One might think that traders, private investors, and institutions had yet to arrive at the age of reason by the way they obstinately cling to every inch of immediate profit maximization at the expense of a foot in deferred wealth.

PRI signatories are still wondering if the ESG criteria they have committed to taking into account are "material": that is, whether they have an impact on stock price. The question is fundamentally absurd. Obviously, social, environmental, and good governance criteria are "material." Climate change, for instance, carries an astronomical price tag. The depletion of natural resources and losses to biodiversity will imperil our economic system. Contempt for human rights across the supply chains that result in the products we buy and consume erodes the foundations of our democracies. Governance entirely directed toward increasing the wealth of shareholders has a devastating effect on the social contract that, among other things, binds the company to the general good. Granted, these costs will not come due for another 20 or 50 years. But how long is 50 years? Set against the scale of our civilization's history, it's practically tomorrow. In finance, however, 50 years is the far-distant future: well beyond what finance professionals refer to as the "long term," generally situated in the vicinity of eight years.

There is a zero-principle missing from the PRI, one that needs to be recognized before asking investors to incorporate ESG issues into their decision-making. This foundational principle would demand that "long-term investors," so called because they have long-term liabilities (this includes insurers, sovereign wealth funds, pension funds, etc.), actually behave like long-term investors! The idea is not to replace the current cult of short-term thinking with a dictatorship of the long term, but to balance the forces at work: let those whose obligations are long-term invest in the long term. At the moment we are a long way from such a balance.

The most frequent decisions made (or delegated) by these allegedly long-term investors are:

- No decisions: this consists of constantly comparing funds to market indices, a logic sometimes pushed to the absurdity of instantly replicating such indices;

- Decisions based on expectations of how the market will behave in a horizon of three months or less, sometimes days, and rarely extending beyond the year's end.

Without the aforementioned foundational principle, incorporating ESG criteria in the investment process becomes an act of faith. And as we know, faith is hard to come by. In practice, signatories' commitment runs the risk of being superficial, unlikely to have much impact on investment decisions or, by extension, on the economy.

Taking into account social and environmental impact requires that traders, savers, pension funds, corporations, and institutional investors reconnect with a culture of investment. This means making thoughtful decisions about which companies, people, and projects to support. That every individual have access to the financial markets via an online trading site may well be a good thing; however, the economy needs to maintain conduits for channeling savings toward the long term. Banks, which historically played this role, transforming short-term deposits into long-term loans, have seen their role in financing decline to the advantage of the financial markets. It is therefore essential that the latter assume these responsibilities.

However, if the exponential growth of assets managed by PRI signatories does not appear to encourage better incorporation of sustainable development issues, it is also because some see Responsible Investment as a specialty reserved for technical experts. Others perceive it as a dubious marketing concept, leading many to lose sight of SRI's real objectives. The goal of SRI is *not* to "integrate ESG criteria," but to act in ways that promote sustainable development. In order to have any chance of reaching this goal, the Socially Responsible Investment industry needs to make significant progress on several fronts.

Actually implementing Responsible Investment practices

Step one: know what we're talking about. Here, it is worth pointing out the work that has been done in France by the SRI commission of the French association of financial management professionals, AFG and the FIR.[1] By adopting a definition of SRI grounded in its goals ("contribute to sustainable development"), rather than particular means of attaining them (integrating ESG criteria), these SRI professionals contribute to changing the current paradigm:

> SRI (Socially Responsible Investment) entails placing funds in order to achieve social and environmental impact by financing businesses and public entities that contribute to

---

1   AFG stands for *Association française de la gestion financière* (French Association of Asset Management Professionals). The FIR is the *Forum pour l'Investissement Responsable* (Responsible Investment Forum).

sustainable development, whatever their sector of activity. By influencing the governance and behavior of economic actors, SRI promotes a responsible economy.[2]

Revising the methods employed by extra-financial ratings agencies

The role played by financial ratings agencies (primarily S&P, Moody's, and Fitch), or, more precisely, the disproportionate importance accorded such ratings by investors, is undoubtedly an aggravating factor when it comes to the financial crisis. This is why it is so important that the voice of what is known as extra-financial analysis be heard clearly in parallel in order to provide a counterweight to the financial agencies.

This is far from being the case, despite the emergence of major players such as MSCI, Sustainalytics, or Vigeo. These agencies attempt to provide qualitative evaluations of the measures taken by management at businesses seeking to improve their CSR. However, extra-financial ratings agencies still lag in terms of incorporating social and environmental performance. That is to say, they place more weight on good intentions than on performance expectations or achievements. Clearly, ratings agencies have fallen prey to confusion between means and ends, or, to put it even more bluntly, between words and deeds.

These ratings have fueled bewilderment. Frequently, large multinationals that have a negative impact on the environment

---

2   See the AFG's July 2, 2013 press release, "L'ISR adopte une nouvelle définition afin de mieux se faire connaître des épargnants." Available at www.afg.asso.fr/index.php?option=com_content&view=article&id =4894%3Alisr-adopte-une-nouvelle-definition-afin-de-mieux-se-faire-connaitre-des-epargnants-&catid=516%3A2013&lang=fr,   accessed October 22, 2015.

but publish extensive reports devoted to their sustainable development policies wind up with a better rating than small companies whose business is products with indisputable environmental benefits, but which lack the time or the means to produce a carbon accounting report. A reform of the methods used by these extra-financial agencies is thus crucial to the credibility of SRI.

Better evaluating governance

When it comes to ESG criteria, the first two letters—standing for environmental and social—seem fairly straightforward; the third, which stands for governance, somewhat less so. What is the relationship between corporate governance and solutions to the social and environmental issues facing our era? Why is good governance a prerequisite for SRI investors? Historically, corporate governance is a theme that grew out of the movement in favor of shareholder democracy, in order to protect the interests of minority shareholders. Certain SRI managers cling to this shareholder-oriented view.

The fact is, good governance—or, let us say, responsible governance—cannot be content to align the interests of management with those of shareholders exclusively. Governance must seek to align the interests of all stakeholders with the societal object, aka mission, of the company, which cannot, by definition, be separated from the general interest. This is the view of Jack Welch, former CEO of General Electric, for whom the concept of "shareholder value is the stupidest thing in the world; shareholder value is an outcome, not a strategy."[3]

---

3   Francesco Guerrera, "Welch condemns share price focus," *Financial Times,* March 12, 2009.

As work by the Cercle des Bernardins has recently demonstrated,[4] a business is not a "faceless corporation." Ultimately, it will be necessary to dismantle Corporate Governance to establish *Company* Governance. This shift in corporate culture can be encouraged by regulatory innovations, like those that create new types of enterprise, such as the *Benefit Corporations* that have appeared in the United States.[5] It also requires that shareholders shoulder their responsibilities. Shareholding confers certain rights, true, but not unbridled license. A responsible shareholder must act in the interests of the business when exercising voting rights, participating in dialogue and engaging with companies. Somewhere between the (many) passive shareholders who fail to exercise their voting rights, and the activist shareholders whose only strategy is to maximize short-term shareholder value, there must be a third way. It is up to SRI to discover and reinforce this alternative path.

Relying on measurable indicators

And last but by no means least, SRI needs to prove that it produces value-added social and environmental outcomes. Many investors lack confidence in Responsible Investment simply because they have doubts about its effectiveness. Granted, not

4   See the Cercle des Bernardins seminar of April 29–30, 2011: "L'entreprise comme dispositif de creation collective: Vers un nouveau type de contrat collectif" ("The Corporation as an Entity for Collective Creation: Forging a New Type of Social Contract"); www.collegedesbernardins.fr/images/pdf/Recherche/2/recherche09-11/colloque/5_entreprisecommedispositif.pdf, accessed October 22, 2015.

5   A Benefit Corporation, also called a B-Corp, is a form of business enterprise recognized by 28 of the 50 United States. While Benefit Corporations are run for profit, they also include positive social and environmental outcomes as part of their legally defined goals.

everything can be measured, much less monetized; nonetheless, the successful development of SRI necessarily entails relevant quantitative indicators—tons of carbon avoided, number of jobs created, and so on—as well as better corporate communication on the topic of their CSR policies and goals. Businesses are now subject to considerable obligations in terms of transparency. This is true both in France (article 225 of the *Loi Grenelle* pertaining to corporate disclosure of social and environmental information), and also at the European level, since the 2014 directive requiring large companies to publish non-financial and corporate governance data.[6]

However, these demands for greater reporting have yet to be reflected in corporations' communications strategies, which continue to focus almost entirely on financial data, despite the fact that many CEOs and finance professionals admit that quarterly reports are of little value. Not only are such documents extremely time-consuming to produce, they often wreak havoc on stock prices. This was one of the principal conclusions of the Kay Review of 2012.[7] Might one not profitably replace these onerous and by nature short-termist publications with an annual period for communicating on the financial and extra-financial situation of companies? This would provide an opportunity for

6   Directive 2014/95/EU on disclosure of non-financial and diversity information by certain large undertakings and groups (eur-lex. europa.eu/legal-content/EN/TXT/?uri=CELEX:32014L0095) amends Accounting Directive 2013/34/EU (eur-lex.europa.eu/legal-content/EN/ TXT/?uri=CELEX:32013L0034). It requires companies to disclose, in their management report, information on policies, risks, and outcomes as regards environmental matters, social and employee aspects, respect for human rights, anti-corruption and bribery issues, and diversity in their board of directors. See ec.europa.eu/finance/accounting/ non-financial_reporting/index_en.htm.

7   See note 5 on page 19.

responsible investors and businesses to discuss issues with a view to improving their respective practices, particularly in the area of reporting.

Murmurs to this effect are beginning to be heard on the international stage: the International Integrated Reporting Council (IIRC) promotes a global and strategic vision of businesses in order to eliminate the unrealistic contrast between financial reports, on the one hand, and "sustainable development" data on the other. In the meantime, however, we needn't wait for the implementation of flawless reporting; why not, for instance, require carbon tracking in high-impact sectors? What excuses are there for the paucity of reporting on social issues, such as numbers and distribution of jobs, total salaried employees, net job creation, etc.? Publishing such information could also be demanded of exchange-listed companies. Gaining access to household savings to satisfy financing requirements is a major advantage for companies, for which, in return, full and detailed reporting hardly seems unreasonable.

Investing in sustainable development

Taking action for the environment and society is a noble cause, certainly. However, many investors are still wondering whether, at the end of the day, SRI creates wealth for households. Once again, let us recall here that ethical considerations and financial returns are of different orders, and thus not comparable. What argument—unless perhaps cultural or religious belief—is going to sway those human beings who genuinely believe they would be happier with a few million in cash, easily gained, even knowing that this came at the expense of humanity's collective wealth, their own life expectancy, or the well-being of their children to come? By the same token, why would a shareholder be interested in creating long-term value for a business if able to dodge in and out of its capital at will and quasi-instantaneously?

Empirical research has tried to find a statistical answer to the question of SRI performance. However, studies are tripped up by the multiplicity and variety of methodologies. For instance, it is practically impossible to compare the performance of an SRI fund based on "exclusion" (which avoids investing in certain industries like tobacco or arms) with that of a "best-in-class" fund, which selects those companies exhibiting the best practices within their sector, but without excluding any industry as a whole? In any event, the investigation has so far yielded the unsurprising conclusion that there is no significant difference in performance between SRI funds and more traditional counterparts. It would thus be very tenuous to claim any correlation between valuation and the quality of companies' CSR policies, or, by extension, between SRI management and financial performance. Does this mean there is no relationship between expected financial return and SRI management and that one is condemned to choose between ethics and returns or subordinate one to the other? Probably not.

Investing in the economy to come

Because they are grounded on physical realities—population demographics, climate change, and depletion of natural resources to cite a few—sustainable development issues will have deep and lasting impacts on the way our economies function. These changes will require new regulations and changes in consumer behavior. Companies that have taken these issues into account in their industrial processes and innovation strategy will have a significant competitive advantage for quite some time. In other words, while sustainable development certainly has an ethical foundation, it is also bound up with practical and material changes shaping our societies. Like any transformation, it involves risks that need to be avoided or minimized and also opportunities. Seen in this light, SRI is to be understood less as the practical application of an ethical position that seeks to separate the wheat from the chaff on the basis of some *a priori* and eternal truths, and more as an adaptive process that dynamically seeks to encourage investment in those projects offering the best fit with sustainable future growth. Despite being of distinctly different orders, ethical and financial preoccupations are intertwined, and are, in fact, reconcilable.

The fact that SRI takes many forms makes it somewhat difficult for the broader public to grasp, and can trip up professionals as well. This smorgasbord of methods can be schematically grouped into three categories according to the ability of each to create ethical and/or financial value.

TABLE 1: **Typology of SRI investment strategies**

SRI process	Ethical value created	Financial value created
ESG engagement Via constructive ongoing dialogue with corporations, investors seek to effect improvements in the ESG behaviors of the businesses they invest in.	Outcomes of engagement with companies. Capacity of investors to meaningfully influence the business practices of companies, particularly those exposed to significant social or environmental risks.	In most cases, the financial value created is minimal, as the process aims only to avert potential ESG risks. In some cases a considerable financial return can be expected in the long term, where results serve to catalyze a change of business model that takes sustainable development into account.
ESG selectivity This involves fixing a minimum threshold of ESG quality below which a company is not an eligible investment. Investors select companies as a function of their ESG behaviors.	Varies according to the ESG quality threshold employed and average ESG quality of the portfolio. Selection may be more or less stringent. Tendency to exhibit sectorial bias that deviates from reference indices (choosing more virtuous sectors).	Potentially positive financially, but more likely to be negative. While this selection process helps avoid ESG risks, it often prevents managers from taking advantage of financially attractive opportunities that fail to meet ESG criteria.
Thematic ESG approach Investors seek to prioritize investment in companies whose products, processes, and strategic plan reflect awareness of sustainable development issues.	Varies according to the ESG quality threshold employed and average ESG quality of the portfolio. Selection may be more or less stringent. Presence in the portfolio of assets whose revenues (or investments) contribute sufficiently to addressing the challenges of sustainable development and whose ESG risks are appropriately controlled.	In most cases, highly favorable over a long-term investment cycle (eight years), as securities are selected only where they present attractive growth potential.

Prioritizing a thematic approach

A thematic SRI portfolio investing in corporate stocks or bonds consists entirely of projects that are sensitive to, or actively addressing, sustainability issues and whose fundamentals reveal a potential for long-term returns. This is by far the most promising approach in terms of performance, both financial and ethical. It combines risk reduction with identifying opportunities. A business's ESG quality and the strategy it pursues in terms of products and services are at the heart of the asset manager's security selection process, relieving the portfolio of the need to adhere to a benchmark.

Thematic management is the exact opposite of the "best-in-class" methodology currently most prevalent. What exactly is a best-in-class methodology? Most SRI managers apply an "ESG filter" of sorts that screens their investment universe. This eliminates some number of companies (varyingly sizeable), whose CSR does not meet the filter's quality standards. In order to ensure they are present in all sectors, investors apply the filter industry by industry, rather than to the universe as a whole. This approach has obvious flaws making it ill fitted to massively direct savings toward the industries of tomorrow, since it merely reproduces the status quo by selecting those corporations whose behavior is considered the most acceptable. The method is equally unsound from a financial perspective. *A priori* filtering is generally experienced by asset managers as an irksome constraint, either because it nudges them away from their benchmark index, or because it places out of reach a certain number of companies with seductive financial profiles.

A management style focused on environmental and social innovation can outperform in the medium term. The founding logic of SRI involves recognizing that money is *not*, in fact, neutral, and that allocating capital to this or that company, project, etc. actually contributes to shaping its potential for growth. SRI is needed, not only to finance sustainable projects, but also to create the conditions under which a sustainable economy is possible.

For those who are concerned about their retirement savings—therefore interested in achieving long-term gains and generally favorable to a sustainable economy that can encourage future generations to support the current ones—the principal attraction of SRI lies in its ability to contribute to a stronger economy down the road. This is the underlying and essential message we want to convey to individuals, investors, and asset managers who are currently trying to beat market indices. An index doesn't come out of nowhere: it represents the economy at a particular moment, like a snapshot. A much more relevant approach for a saver would be to adopt a method of investing which would, if broadly shared, reinforce the economy as a whole. SRI provides performance the way knowledge does—a sustainable economy will always offer better outcomes than an economy wrestling with the disastrous effects of climate change, just as a knowledge economy will always be more profitable than an economy of ignorance.

What does this mean in concrete terms?

Investing means making choices to intelligently allocate available capital, and actively engaging in a management process. It is worth mentioning here that besides the indices "everyone" follows—the S&P 500, the EuroStoxx 50, the FTSE 100, or the CAC 40—there is a growing number of indices that do not seek to represent the state of the market (the status quo), but rather an investment style, or aim (the world as we see it or want it to become). These indices are comprised of companies combining individual performance and collective well-being that contribute to a circular economy, are sparing in terms of CO_2, and promote the general welfare, in particular that of stakeholders. This is what we attempted to do in our "Sustainable Equities" index.[8]

A new way to invest

Two questions guided us in designing this index:

- What kind of companies do we want to invest in?

- What are the risks we are not prepared to take?

As for the first question, the businesses we would like to invest in are those producing or distributing products and services with high levels of social and environmental utility. These are often innovative companies. They are positioned in high-growth markets, like producers of electric batteries, or new materials: for instance, those permitting vehicle lightweighting; E-learning, recycling and waste management, decontamination, and "green" fertilizers are other examples from this long list. Thus, companies whose core business is developing renewable energy and most companies within the healthcare sector claim the highest rankings on this scale, in contrast to corporations that extract and sell fossil fuels or commercialize tobacco. For sectors whose

8   The "Sustainable Equities" index is organized by the French asset management firm Mirova, and has been published by Euronext since April 2014. The index consists of Large Cap companies listed on European exchanges that are selected by Mirova's ESG research team; https://www.euronext.com/products/indices/FR0011710326-XPAR/market-information, accessed October 26, 2015.

impact is less stark, rankings are relative and depend on the degree of usefulness or innovation each company exhibits in its domain. Only the highest-rated 20% of all companies are considered eligible for our index. Since the economy must imperatively become sustainable, it is in our interest to allocate capital to these. Here, the word "interest" should be understood as comprising two broad categories:

1. As citizens, it is in our interest for our investments to promote companies compatible with a sustainable economy.

2. As individuals looking to maximize our savings, it is in our interest to invest our money in companies with the potential to be winners in the world of tomorrow.

As regards risk, some of the dangers we are not willing to envisage are financial: companies whose economic performance is too weak, whose debt is excessive, whose solvency or liquidity is questionable. Other concerns are extra-financial: no company would be considered that failed to respect fundamental human rights or whose business ethics were found wanting. Eighty-four companies, drawn from all sectors of the economy, made the cut. Only the financial industry is absent. The products and services currently offered at this time do not, sadly, meet our criteria.

The importance we place on relatively small and intermediate-sized businesses in our index is the main feature that differentiates it from most market indices. According to the most commonly accepted definition, a "large company" is one whose market capitalization exceeds a billion euros. There are approximately a thousand such entities listed on Europe's exchanges alone. Yet, for the most part, traditional indices consist of firms whose capitalizations are many times larger. The same term is used to designate corporations valued at a billion euros, and those worth a hundred billion. To complicate things, the weighting of a company in most market indices depends on its market capitalization! So our go-to market indices are really affected primarily by the largest companies. These are the same indices that serve as reference points for managers of stock portfolios and, in the case of index-tracking, dictate the portfolio itself. As a result, a significant portion of savings are mechanically and without thought directed toward companies on the basis of their market cap. The lion's share of investment flows toward companies that are already gigantic. Once again, the world that prevailed yesterday does more to serve the financial markets than it does for the world of tomorrow.

The need to champion small and medium-sized businesses is a major talking point for elected officials in many European countries. Why, then, is it that this passive drain of resource allocation toward the largest industrial groups goes unmentioned? The only initiatives to date have been aimed at creating savings vehicles for a "niche market," and benefit extremely small companies. France's *Plan d'épargne en actions-PME* (SME equity savings scheme), or PEA-PME, established in January of 2014, is one example. But very small businesses are not really in need of attention from the investment community—retail banks are more likely to prove useful. Instead, it is often the density of mid-sized firms that puts the commercial and industrial "spring" in an economy—Germany's, for instance. These are corporations large enough to absorb the considerable drain on resources associated with being listed on an exchange (notably the associated reporting costs) and those most likely to benefit from increased access to financial capital.

Looking back over the experience of designing a universe of securities from which to draw our index, we can affirm that it is indeed possible to create balanced portfolios that are consistent with the concept of sustainable growth. The role of investors is not to replicate the world that exists, but to shape the world to come: investing means looking down the road, not gazing into the rearview mirror. Such an allocation of capital is possible, it is necessary, and it is useful for the market and the economy.

The progressive incorporation of some level of ESG criteria, which many asset management companies practice at this point, is an encouraging trend. However, it by no means suffices. Responsible Investment needs to prove that it produces real impact, some form of social or environmental value-added that makes sense to savers. The value involved remains difficult for the broader public to grasp so long as evaluations focus on the behavior or CSR policies of large companies. Investors need simpler messages that are clear. This is one reason funds have sprung up that focus more specifically on projects rather than companies, or invest in smaller companies where environmental or social benefits are easier to comprehend

FIGURE 3: **Comparative breakdown by market cap of companies represented in the Stoxx 600 and Mirova SI Europe indices**

Source: Mirova/Euronext

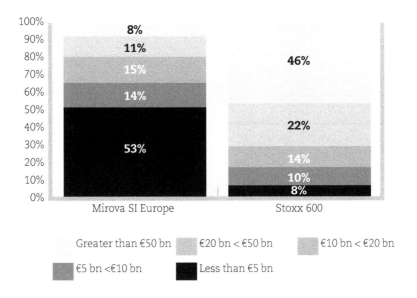

A lever for transforming businesses
=====

SRI can be a powerful tool for inciting, accelerating, and accompanying changes in companies' CSR policies. When corporate executives meet with extra-financial analysts, they always ask: "Do our CSR decisions really influence your investment choices?" When ESG analysts answer in the affirmative, it clearly modifies the implicit duty that investors entrust to management. This is probably the single best way to strengthen the CSR practices that executives implement.

SRI follows a circular, rather than a linear logic. Sustainable development issues justify the implementation of CSR policies,

which, in turn, invite SRI management. This type of management goads companies into improving their CSR, thereby allow-
ing these same companies to better address sustainability issues.

4

Harnessing savings to transform the economy

It is a mistake to believe that sweeping public-sector incentives, be they regulatory or fiscal, are needed to create financial ecosystems favorable to sustainability. Sometimes weak signals are sufficient. Without revolutionizing the way our markets work we can nonetheless use them differently, simply by focusing on the long term.

Three main avenues leading to innovative savings are:

- Financing infrastructure and social programs via new kinds of partnerships between public and private sectors;

- Better channeling savings: that is, directing them toward desirable projects, notably thanks to transparent reporting (green bonds, impact bonds, social impact bonds);

- Financing new economic models based on microfinance, addressing the needs of the bottom of the pyramid, and promoting inclusive finance, as well as, more broadly speaking, what is called the social economy.

In this manner, savings can contribute to transforming the economy itself.

New partnerships between the public and private sectors

Public financing as a source of leverage

As a result of ballooning sovereign debt, states are more and more withdrawing from financing infrastructure, including public transportation, airports, power and sanitation facilities, hospitals, and prisons. Such investments have been what we call "privatized." This is by no means a new idea. During the Industrial Revolution, the development of transportation networks in Western countries was essentially fueled by private initiatives. In France, the Paris sanitation and water utilities were financed during the 19th century by the issue of debt instruments that would today qualify as "green bonds."[1]

Today, we need to:

- Renew investment in infrastructure to accelerate economic recovery;

- Find alternatives to public funds for financing infrastructure;

---

1   Olivier Crespi Reghizzi, "The financing history of urban water infrastructure in Paris (1807–1925): Lessons from the past to enlighten present and future challenges?" Department of Economics, Management and Quantitative Methods at Università degli Studi di Milano Departmental Working Papers no. 2012-22 (2012); https://ideas.repec.org/p/mil/wpdepa/2012-22.html, accessed June 5, 2014.

- Direct these investments toward projects with positive social and environmental advantages.

Our financial innovations must be driven by a clear intent to combine these three elements.

A number of programs have been launched, some national, others European or global, to nudge long-term investments towards these infrastructure needs. Some emphasize public funds, others private financing, but all agree that only a combination of the two can hope to prove efficient.

The most iconic of these initiatives is surely the *Green Paper on Long-term Financing of the European Economy*, published by the European Commission in 2013. The preface to the document sets out the issues only too clearly: "Europe urgently needs to get back to intelligent growth that is sustainable and inclusive." The Commission's report observes that "the financial crisis has reduced the ability of the financial sector in Europe to channel savings into long term investment needs."[2] The report insists on the relationship between funding arrangements and the goals of sustainable development: "Long term financing must be achieved in tandem with structural reforms to assist in putting the economy back on track toward sustainable growth." Among the measures suggested in the Green Paper is the creation of a new investment vehicle: The "European Long Term Investment Funds" (ELTIF), designed to encourage institutional investors and individual savers to participate in projects with a financing horizon longer than five years.

---

2   It is worth noting that this observation is, quite rightly, not exclusive to the sovereign debt crisis. The document points out that the whole of the financing circuit is frozen, and highlights increasing fragility in the banking sector as well as risk aversion on the part of savers.

Also worth mentioning here is the G20 plan, adopted at the September 2013 Summit in Saint Petersburg. Its objective is to channel a larger portion of world savings into long-term financing needs, strengthen the environment and guarantees surrounding such investments, and improve the financial structuring of projects. The G20 had already empaneled an international working group whose aim was to prioritize those projects with the strongest showing from a social and environmental perspective. The panel especially emphasized the importance of promoting "pro-poor infrastructures" to ensure access to basic services for the most vulnerable populations, as well as overall employment and small and medium enterprise (SMEs) in developing regions.

Inciting the private sector to participate

More broadly, it behooves us to look at what role public authorities have to play. How can we optimize the actions of governments and supranational institutions? What action can these entities take to influence the choices and behavior of private investors and savers? How can private financing be harnessed to serve large-scale endeavors for the public good? Or, to put it differently, how can we ensure that the financial withdrawal of states is not made at the expense of the public good?

Clearly this can come about only through a renewal of Public–Private Partnerships. "We believe there exist win–win situations . . . where private-sector investors will make money, where governments will be successful in building the kind of infrastructure they need to grow, and the creation of jobs will lift people out of poverty," forcefully claimed Dr. Kim, the president of the World Bank, in September of 2013.[3]

The ministers belonging to the "Green Growth Group"[4] insist on the fact that investments in the energy transition are perfectly compatible with reducing public deficits, insofar as such investments are largely long-term engagements on the part of private-sector actors, particularly European institutional investors, who are collectively responsible for a non-negligible €13.8 trillion in assets, a total equivalent to Europe's annual GDP. The affirmation is true; however, via fiscal mechanisms, carbon pricing and subsidization, public finance remains at the heart of efforts to finance the energy transition and mobilize private funds.

A number of institutional investors in Denmark (Pension-Danmark, PKA, DanskVaekstkapital), for instance, have announced the launch of a fund called the Danish Climate Investment Fund:[5] DKK1.2 billion Danish kroner (approximately €150 million) are invested as equity in renewable energy infrastructure, energy efficiency, and public transportation in

3   Natasha Brereton-Fukui, "World Bank to set up global infrastructure facility," *The Wall Street Journal*, September 6, 2013; www.wsj.com/articles/SB10001424127887324577304579058660663794356, accessed November 19, 2015.

4   The Green Growth Group is an informal group of 13 European Ministers of the Environment who share similar ideas regarding energy, climate change, and environmental issues. The countries represented are Belgium, Denmark, Estonia, Finland, France, Germany, Italy, the Netherlands, Portugal, Slovenia, Spain, Sweden, and the United Kingdom; "Going for Green Growth: The case for ambitious and immediate EU low carbon action," October 28, 2013; www.gov.uk/government/publications/going-for-green-growth-the-case-for-ambitious-and-immediate-eu-low-carbon-action, accessed April 25, 2015.

5   Press release announcing the creation of the Danish Climate Fund: www.ifu.dk/en/service/news-and-publications/news/new-climate-investment-agreement-worth-billions, accessed November 24, 2015.

developing countries, as well as in projects for adaptation to the consequences of climate change. The initiative is 40% funded by the Danish government, with private investors providing the remaining 60%. If we include bank loans, these capital investments will make it possible to finance some €1 billion worth of new projects. Expected return is 12%. This Public–Private Partnership permits the realization of several distinct objectives:

- Offering Danish pension funds investments with a favorable return, and thus improving the pension of future Danish retirees;

- Contributing to Denmark's external policies and the country's development while combating climate change;

- Supporting exports by Danish companies, particularly those involved in technologies associated with renewable energy.

Infrastructure, certainly, but what kind?

The construction of large-scale facilities can sometimes have unintended collateral effects that are deleterious, socially or environmentally. Intensifying public transportation and communications networks in cities and coastal or industrial areas tends, for example, to exacerbate inequalities between those who are connected and those left out. At times, even the choices of supranational institutions can be questionable, as indicated by the regrettable fact that a significant portion of all financing supplied by the European Investment Bank (EIB) still goes to projects for high-speed motorways in western Europe.

So, beyond the level of investment, we must also look carefully at the arbitrage among different investments. These are choices, and therefore, consequently, it is appropriate to make certain choices more attractive than others. The economist Edward Gramlich affirms that "it is not enough merely to increase public spending levels, but to invest in the right projects and better manage such investments."[6] Similarly, Pierre Ducret, Director of the French think-tank CDC Climate Research,[7] remarks that "financing isn't what promotes, change, it's the competition between projects looking to be financed that does."

So, what should be financed? How do we set priorities? Current debates over the energy transition demonstrate that there can be significant divergences between the perspective of industry—largely corporatist—and the expectations of civil society or NGOs. The ecological and social issues at stake are obscured by strictly economic considerations. For instance, "What's the use, in carpeting our landscape in space-consuming photovoltaic or wind farms when industrial production of the former is completely dominated by the Chinese?" asks Michel Rousseau, economist and president of the Fondation Concorde.[8] Any time the issue of financing comes up, it is natural to ask

6   Edward M. Gramlich, "Infrastructure Investment: A Review Essay," *Journal of Economic Literature* 32 (September 1994). Available at www1.worldbank.org/publicsector/pe/pfma07/EdwardGramlich.pdf, accessed November 24, 2015.

7   CDC Climate Research is a wholly owned subsidiary of the Caisse des Dépôts created in 2010 to provide a forum for research and debate on issues related to climate change. Since 2013, the Caisse des Dépôts has made climate its top strategic priority.

8   Michel Rousseau, "Transition énergétique: il est urgent d'attendre!" *La Tribune*,   May   28,   2013;   www.latribune.fr/opinions/ tribunes/20130528trib000766862/transition-energetique-il-est-urgent-d-attendre.html, accessed October 22, 2015. The Fondation Concorde is an independently funded French think-tank that brings together academic researchers and business leaders to debate contemporary issues and devise potential solutions, which are submitted to government authorities. Its principal preoccupation is the economic health of France.

about how relevant the proposed investment is. But answering that question is not necessarily simple; it requires a reliable methodology, preferably one that is public and widely shared. Private actors have recently taken tentative first steps toward measuring and assessing the environmental and social impact of infrastructure projects.[9]

Evaluating impact requires highly developed skills, and is an expertise in its own right. According to the sector (social amenities, energy utilities, transportation) and geographic location (developed vs. developing countries), infrastructure projects will look very different, and cannot therefore be evaluated in the same ways. It is also necessary to consider the entire value chain implicated in a project, from its development and construction through its operational life. It is not enough to distinguish between a rail project and a plan to build highways; good practices need to be identified and recognized, such as protection for biodiversity, energy efficiency, and less energy-intensive mobility solutions, such as ride-sharing. Also, the actual impact of the facilities that result needs to be examined. Lastly, assessments ought to incorporate both quantitative criteria (CO_2, kWh, number of jobs created, total budget allocated to preventative or palliative measures), and qualitative evaluation (quality of jobs, level of engagement). Just because a project is financing the production of renewable energy doesn't mean one can ignore its consequences. A wind farm's considerable footprint requires arbitrage between energy and agricultural production, bearing in mind that projects have to be acceptable to local communities.

---

9   The Asset management company Mirova, in partnership with responsible consulting firm BeCitizen, has developed a methodology for analyzing the social and environmental impact of infrastructure projects.

All in all, it is clear that a need for a green infrastructure label is needed. True, we already have the "Equator Principles"[10] which are designed to avert as many negative impacts on ecosystems and communities as possible. However, such declarations of intent are by no means sufficient. A formal mechanism is required for incorporating environmental and social criteria into infrastructure projects.

As early as 2008, the UN devoted a report to the governance of Public–Private Partnerships (PPPs), which pointed out their potential to address social and environmental concerns when properly managed in their development phase, including Environmental Impact Assessment (EIA).[11] A report produced in 2013 for the French government, *Pour une économie positive* (*For a Positive Economy*),[12] emphasized the importance of transforming these contracts to make them effective mechanisms for inducing positive change. The idea proposed in the document revolves around incorporating environmental and social impact criteria upstream, while preserving the existing mechanics of partnerships: that is to say, a global contract including both construction and maintenance. Among other measures, minimum thresholds would be set to ensure participation by SMEs, thereby

---

10 The Equator Principles (EPs) is a risk management framework, adopted by financial institutions, for determining, assessing, and managing environmental and social risk in projects and is primarily intended to provide a minimum standard for due diligence to support responsible risk decision-making.

11 *Guidebook on Promoting Good Governance in Public–Private Partnerships* (Geneva: United Nations Economic Commission for Europe, 2008); www.unece.org/fileadmin/DAM/ceci/publications/ppp.pdf, accessed June 10, 2015.

12 Working group chaired by Jacques Attali, *Pour une économie positive* (Paris: Éditions Fayard, 2013). Available at www.ladocumentationfrancaise.fr/var/storage/rapports-publics/134000625.pdf.

reinforcing local businesses, ambitious goals in terms of energy efficiency for every project so as to contribute to national and European-wide objectives, firm commitments to job creation and to inclusive diversity above and beyond regulatory compliance, governance procedures that better implicate the full range of stakeholders in evaluations, and, last but not least, rigorous monitoring of social and environmental impact throughout a project's life-cycle. A report by the World Bank, also in 2013, struck a similar note. *Green Infrastructure Finance: A Public–Private Partnership Approach to Climate Finance* focused on the potential use of PPP as an effective tool for funding much-needed investments in GHG emissions reduction and climate change adaptation measures.

Just how important is financing infrastructure?

The economic difficulties that have dogged the world since 2008 initially had a delaying effect, pushing subjects related to the environment and climate change to the sidelines along with the struggle against poverty. In the face of teetering financial equilibrium, a disoriented banking system and social impacts that affected developed countries, the long term got the short end of the proverbial stick, as manifest in stalled international negotiations, and the first reduction since 1997, of the funds allocated to development aid, which shrank 2.7% in 2011 as compared to 2010.

Likewise, the absolute priority having been to inject growth back into the global economy, the energy transition seemed to fade into the background. While in some countries (France and

South Korea[13] stand out here), some portion of initiatives involved green growth, others, like the United Kingdom, focused on bank bailouts and reigniting consumption. The financial crisis also slowed down the development of renewable energy. According to Bloomberg Energy Watch, investment in green energy amounted to €267.8 billion in 2012 worldwide—11% less than in 2011 (€302.3 billion). The good news is that this initial phase of defensive recoil appears to be behind us. In January of 2015, Bloomberg reported that clean energy investment had risen 16% despite the collapse of oil prices, which many believed would be a barrier to investment in alternative energy.[14] The interdependence among infrastructure development, social, or environmental objectives, and economic growth are better and better understood. As Patricia Crifo of France's elite École Polytechnique puts it: "The double crisis, economic and financial on the one hand, ecological on the other, positions issues of sustainable development at the core of our market economies and highlights the need to restore the conditions necessary for long-term growth."[15] A consensus is beginning to coalesce

13   "The 'Green New Deal' project, announced in the wake of the global financial crisis in January 2009, is a green investment programme designed as a means to help overcome the crisis and actively respond to international energy and environmental issues. It aims to promote green growth based on low carbon energy and energy efficiency, generate new jobs to revitalize the economy." Remarks made by Kim Choong-soo, South Korea's ambassador to the OECD during the 8th Korea–France Forum, May 11, 2009 (informal translation available on the Korea Foundation website).

14   Louise Downing, "Clean energy investment jumps 16%, shaking off oil's drop", *Bloomberg News,* January 9, 2015. Available at www.bloomberg.com/news/articles/2015-01-09/clean-energy-investment-jumps-16-on-china-s-support-for-solar, accessed August 4, 2015.

15   Patricia Crifo, "L'Économie Verte." Special issue *Cahiers Français*, 355 (La documentation française, March/April 2010).

around the theme of long-term investing. It is not only about forestalling or adapting to climate change and demographic growth, but actually a circumstantial necessity. Stimulating investment, especially in major infrastructure projects, appears to offer a way forward in the effort to kick-start growth. Here, risk management and economic opportunity flow together.

Demonstrating the link between economic growth and sustainable development issues is a crucial prerequisite for mobilizing savings and, to this effect, the case of climate change is particularly interesting. The energy transition has become a focal priority, not only among ecologists, or within the international forum provided by the International Panel on Climate Change (IPCC), but a concern at the center of serious economic thought; and even those economic circles least inclined to give credence to such ideas have begun to take heed.

The financing needs of the infrastructures required to make the energy or ecological transition a reality are stupendous. For the UN, "It is well-recognised internationally that high levels of investment in the cost-effective implementation of clean technologies are required to enable the shift towards a sustainable low-carbon global economy . . . Investment must be pledged at a level that exceeds any previous allocation to clean technology implementation by at least an order of magnitude."[16]

Interdependence among quality of infrastructure, competitiveness and growth has been extensively studied, and proven beyond reasonable doubt. Economists have brought to light the relation between public spending on infrastructure and increases in productivity, as well as lower transaction and production

---

16   United Nations, "Climate Change Finance: Introduction"; www.unep. org/climatechange/finance/Introduction/tabid/29540/Default.aspx, accessed August 6, 2015.

costs. Without winding the clock all the way back to Roman aqueducts, the history of the world's great industrial powers is testimony to the intricate connections between large-scale transportation infrastructure and the growth of production. In the United States, the construction of canals in the first years of the 19th century, the explosive development of railroads during the latter half, followed by the rise of a national highway system in the early 1900s, all mark major phases of the country's geographic and commercial development. Improvements to infrastructure lead to economic growth.

Conversely, in emerging economies the absence or inadequacy of such amenities is considered a major bottleneck limiting economic development. Beyond the simple correlation between economic foundations and activity levels, infrastructure can provide solutions to some of the looming environmental and social issues previously mentioned. Population growth and urbanization call for the construction of housing, water and sanitary utilities, transportation and communication infrastructure, all valuable tools in the struggle to eliminate poverty and reduce inequality. Today, close to 800 million human beings have no access to safe drinking water, while more than twice that number cannot count on a reliable supply of energy. Yet, to feed the global population of 9 billion currently estimated for the planet in 2050, water needs are expected to grow by 50%. [17]The issue of global water shortage is exacerbated by declining water tables and the extreme weather events induced by climate change. Social and environmental imbalances run parallel here, mutually amplifying current trends.

---

17   See Mirova/University of Cambridge, *Food Security—Closing the Food Gap: Opportunities for Investment*, February 2015.

The World Bank's website features a question that might appear surprising at first: "How building roads reduce child deaths?"[18] Similarly, the G20 now considers infrastructure projects a crucial mechanism for combating poverty and supporting development. Priorities include energy, drinking water, and sanitation as well as roads, especially in Africa. In *Promoting Pro-poor Growth: Policy Guidance for Donors* (2006), the OECD recognizes that "inadequate or inappropriate economic infrastructure is one of the biggest obstacles to pro-poor growth."[19] The Millennium Development Goals,[20] published in 2000 following the United Nations Millennium summit in Rio, also emphasize infrastructure as a keystone in the struggle against poverty and underdevelopment. According to World Bank estimates, between 800 and 900 million US dollars are invested in infrastructure yearly, yet twice that amount is needed.[21]

And, last but not least, in the struggle against climate change, the correspondingly necessary emergence of renewable energies requires new infrastructure in terms of power production, distribution, and storage. The Green Growth Group estimated in 2013 that investment in electrical power production would grow by 70% in the coming decade.[22] The German energy

---

18 World Bank, "Millennium Development Goals. Goal 4: Reduce Child Mortality by 2015"; www.worldbank.org/mdgs/child_mortality.html, accessed August 8, 2015.

19 OECD, *Pro-poor Growth: Policy Guidelines for Donors*, Part 4, Infrastructure (2006).

20 See the World Bank website: www.worldbank.org.

21 World Bank Group, *Financing for Development Post 2013*; https://www.worldbank.org/content/dam/Worldbank/document/Poverty%20documents/WB-PREM%20financing-for-development-pub-10-11-13web.pdf, accessed October 23, 2015.

22 Green Growth Group, *Going for Green Growth: The Case for Ambitious and Immediate EU Low Carbon Action*, p. 12; https://www.gov.

agency Dena has pointed out a discrepancy between the growth of wind farms and the inadequacy of infrastructure necessary for their functioning, estimating at roughly €56 billion the investments required in this area over the next decade for Germany alone! Nor is adaptation to climate change a concern only for countries in the South. As the Federation of Canadian Municipalities remarks: "in Canada's north, where the impact of climate change is most severe, the infrastructure deficit is expected to double [. . .] as the loss of ice roads costs northern employers millions in transportation costs, while further isolating northern communities."[23]

The *World Energy Outlook* published by the International Energy Agency (IEA) assesses the need for investment in renewable and low-carbon energy at US$25 trillion over the next twenty years, if we are to limit atmospheric CO_2 concentrations to 450 ppm. The Energy–Climate package adopted on January 23, 2008 by the European Commission defined an objective for 2020 known as "3 × 20": 20% reductions in both energy consumption and GHG emissions, alongside a 20% increase in the proportion of renewable energy in the European Union. In March of 2010, the European Commission presented a long-term development strategy called "Europe 2020" designed around a core of priorities that include innovation, via increased research and development efforts, social inclusion, and reinforcing objectives related to the struggle against climate change through the development of "green growth."

uk/government/uploads/system/uploads/attachment_data/file/253029/Green_Growth_Group_Joint_Pamphlet.pdf, accessed November 19, 2015.

23   Federation of Canadian Municipalities, "Climate Change Adaptation"; www.fcm.ca/home/issues/environment/climate-change-adaptation.htm, accessed August 13, 2015.

FIGURE 4: **Breakdown of investments in renewable energy needed in Europe to meet EU 2020 objectives by country**

Source: Mirova/Ernst & Young/freeworldmaps.com

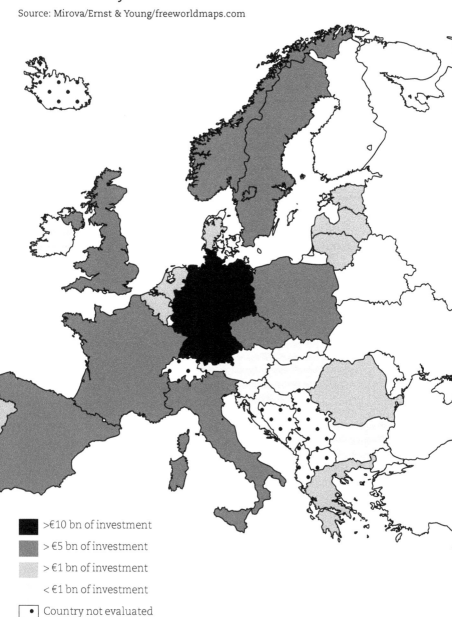

> €10 bn of investment

> €5 bn of investment

> €1 bn of investment

< €1 bn of investment

Country not evaluated

Channeling savings effectively

The ecological transition is an economic issue

The first serious economic analysis to consider the stakes of climate change appeared in October 2006. It was written for the British government by Nicholas Stern, former vice-president of the World Bank. The report's 700 or so pages are devoted to proposing a detailed monetization of the ecological, social, and demographic impacts associated with global warming. In particular, the document evaluates the investments needed to avoid catastrophe and prepare populations for the inevitable effects of climate disruptions (rising sea levels, increasing frequency of extreme weather events, lower agricultural yields). By comparing the cost of inaction with the investment needed, the *Stern Review* seeks to demonstrate that "the cost of preventative measures would be less than that of future risks."[24] To put it differently, solutions would be cost-effective at a macroeconomic level.

The report estimated the potential costs of climate change at around €5.5 trillion (more than the aggregate destruction produced by both World War I and II in the 20th century) if we start immediately. However, this number could be 10 or 20 times higher, according to Stern, if corrective measures were to be delayed. To combat the enormous economic risk, the report proposed that humanity as a whole invest 1% of GDP—€275 billion—in actions aimed at limiting or correcting the effects of climate change. As early as 2008, he admitted to having grossly underestimated the problem.

24   N. Stern, *The Stern Review on the Economics of Climate Change* (London: HM Treasury, October 2006). Available at www.webcitation. org/5nCeyEYJr, accessed June 14, 2014.

While one might quibble with the precise accuracy of the figures, or indeed their relevance, there is no doubt but that the *Stern Report* played an important role in provoking awareness in business circles from the City to Wall Street via the Davos Economic Forum. The energy transition ceased to be a matter of interest only to climatologists and took shape as an economic and financial issue. Ever since, economists have been adding to the piles of analysis, and the relationship between climate change and growth is now extensively studied. Measurement tools are available from some of the world's most serious institutions dedicated to the economy, such as the World Bank, which issued a report in 2014 concluding that a global temperature increase of more than 2°C is likely before the end of the century.[25] The OECD has also published a number of studies on the economics of combating climate change, the cost of adaptation, policy considerations and other similar topics.[26]

Thus, the report certainly provided a much-needed jolt; however, we are still waiting for long-term solutions to appear. Proving the cost of inaction will continue to be a theoretical exercise until we find a way to make financing the energy transition more concretely attractive for investors.

Pointing savings toward the positive economy

Despite the many sermons preached at multilateral conferences, financing for the energy transition and positive infrastructure remains inadequate. The Green Climate Fund, for instance,

---

25   World Bank, "World Is locked into about 1.5°C warming and risks are rising, new climate report finds", November 23, 2014; www.worldbank.org/en/news/feature/2014/11/23/climate-report-finds-temperature-rise-locked-in-risks-rising, accessed November 6, 2015.

26   See the OECD website: www.oecd.org/env/cc, accessed July 23, 2015.

created at the Copenhagen Climate Change Conference (COP15) in 2009, collected only US$10 billion or so in 2015, a drop in the bucket compared to what the *Stern Report* calls for.

Yet the current financial environment should be favorable to such a reallocation. The lower interest rates that have prevailed since the 2008 economic crisis, especially the serious cuts to sovereign debt rates, push institutional investors to seek out other assets offering stable returns at a higher rate over the very long term. These investors have liabilities (retirement payments due in 10, 20, and sometimes 30 or more years) that present interest rates simply don't allow them to meet. Appetite for infrastructure investment, in a wide variety of formats, has never been higher. New infrastructure and debt funds are proliferating, directly financing projects, or buying up long-term debt. According to a half-year report by the specialized data providers Preqin, 63% of international investors would like to increase their holdings in infrastructure.[27]

World savings, particularly pooled household savings in Europe, which are held by pension funds, insurance companies or sovereign wealth funds, do too little to address the most essential issues. Some of the impedance is due to regulations. The European directive "Solvability 2," for instance, demands that insurance companies maintain a higher proportion of cash to cover "risky" investments in stocks or unlisted securities, such as those infrastructure investments. This bias encourages European insurance companies to prefer sovereign bonds! Similar observations might be made about the impact of banking regulations passed in the wake of the financial crisis.[28]

27 Preqin Investor Outlook: Infrastructure, H2 2013; www.preqin.com.
28 The document *Stability and Sustainability in Banking Reform: Are environmental risks missing in Basel III?*, published by the Cambridge

However, procyclic regulations like these, which push economic actors to reduce risk-taking at precisely that moment when the economy most needs investment, are not the only factors to blame. The burden of habit, technical ignorance about these new assets, the difficulty of assessing technological risk, and other similar resistances play a significant part. Financing green growth may be at the center of many banks' communications strategy, but let's not forget that the teams in charge of implementing these projects come from traditional banking, and, not long ago, were busy financing coal-fired power plants. That's not to say that ethical or environmental considerations are necessarily absent from their activity, but they are relegated to the background. The best we can hope for from bankers is rational altruism.

This makes it all the more necessary to render "positive" investments attractive thanks to financial innovation. Public authorities could play a role in this. Unfortunately, grand speeches are many, but actions are few. The European Long Term Investment Funds provide a sobering example. This instrument was created by the European Commission "for putting the European economy on a path of smart, sustainable and inclusive growth . . . for building tomorrow's economy in a way that is less prone to systemic risks and is more resilient."[29] Yet there is no mechanism for controlling whether these funds, the investment horizons of which can stretch to several decades, take into

Institute for Sustainable Development, analyzes how climate issues are factored into post-crisis banking reforms; www.cisl.cam.ac.uk/publications/publication-pdfs/stability-and-sustainability-basel-iii-final-repor.pdf/view.

29   *Official Journal of the European Union* L 123/98 (May 19, 2015). Available at www.cysec.gov.cy/CMSPages/GetFile.aspx?guid=be8af592-a685-4081-a9cf-eda621ca4876.

account the quality of projects' governance or their social and environmental impact. Such elements are not, apparently, investment criteria. To take an extreme example: a fund that invested the entirety of its capital into polluting infrastructure, such as coal-fired power plants, would meet all the eligibility criteria for this new category of funds. There is no mention in the Directive of a single constraint on the type of projects that can be financed!

If public authorities are too slow on the draw, perhaps we should be looking to action initiated by investors themselves. The PRI, discussed in the chapter "Savings as a means of transforming the corporation," is one; however, several new initiatives emerged in 2014 specifically aimed at "decarbonizing" portfolios. Among these are the Montreal Carbon Pledge,[30] sponsored by the PRI, and the Portfolio Decarbonization Coalition, which falls under the aegis of the UNEP-FI.[31] Both of these represent a commitment on the part of signatory investors to calculate and publish the carbon footprint of each portfolio, with the intent of progressively reducing total footprint. Even if there remain some methodological problems to address, such efforts are clearly a step in the right direction.

Green bonds

The instruments known as green bonds[32] are without a doubt the most efficient tool for accelerating investment in the

---

30   See the Montreal Carbon Pledge website: montrealpledge.org.
31   See the UNEP-FI website: unepfi.org/pdc.
32   Some may prefer the term *sustainability bond*, which offers the advantage of encompassing all projects offering direct positive social or environmental impact.

ecological transition, by making it possible to rapidly raise private funds for profitable projects on the basis of carbon credits.[33]

The global bond markets are almost twice the size of their counterparts in equities, with over US$100 trillion in circulation.[34] Furthermore, bonds are the "natural" and preferred investment vehicles for institutional investors, particularly pension funds and insurers, for several reasons:

- They ensure proper coverage of long term liabilities;

- The bond market is very broad and extremely diverse;

- High levels of standardization reduce the processing burden.

So, why, one might ask, invest complex mechanisms or products when the bond market is sitting there? It is broad, liquid, easy to understand, and investors already possess the necessary expertise. No wonder the director of investments at Zurich Invest, which announced in November 2013 that it would make US$1 billion investment in green bonds, considers these to be "low hanging fruit."[35]

---

33 One carbon credit corresponds to a metric ton of carbon dioxide emissions. Each country is entitled to a certain quota of credits. Projects that are CO_2-efficient help economize carbon credits, which can be traded via an international market for the exchange of carbon credits.

34 The $100 trillion Global Debt figure is confirmed by several sources, including Bloomberg and the Bank for International Settlements (BIS) (Branimir Gruić and Andreas Schrimpf, "Cross-border investments in global debt markets since the crisis," BIS, March 9, 2014; www.bis.org/publ/qtrpdf/r_qt1403y.htm). Equity market figures from www.world-exchanges.org/files/2013_WFE_Market_Highlights.pdf.

35 See Novethic Research, *Green and Social Bonds: A Promising Tool*, November 2013. Available at www.novethic.fr/fileadmin/user_upload/tx_ausynovethicetudes/pdf_complets/Green_bonds_report_update_2014.pdf, accessed October 22, 2015.

Where is the green bond market today?

Green bonds *stricto sensu* represented approximately $44 billion at the end of 2014, which is very little if we go by the needs described in the *Stern Report*, or, for that matter, the bond market as a whole. This is obviously a turn-off for investors, who tend to look for high liquidity issues that can be quickly bought and sold at a price that appropriately reflects supply and demand. Nonetheless, this market is growing fast. The total volume of issuance in 2014 amounted to nearly US$27 billion, and, according to Sean Kidney, chairman of the Climate Bonds Initiative (CBI), the market could reach the US$100 billion mark by the end of 2015, although this remains an ambitious target. Such a figure would still not be sufficient, however. Specialists say that the market will need to hit US$200–300 billion in order to achieve adequate liquidity. If true, it means that, as of now, the market still needs to multiply by a factor of four to five. Not at all impossible, according to Christopher Flensborg, of the Scandinavian bank SEB; he believes green bonds will represent 10–15% of all new issuance worldwide within seven years.

FIGURE 5: **Evolution of the market for green and social bonds**

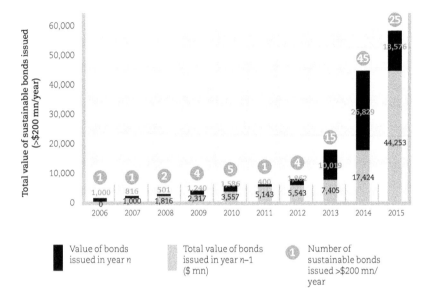

To attract investors, the green bond market also needs a greater variety of issuers offering a broader palette of risk levels and financial returns. Only such diversification can incite financial players to develop the expertise necessary to analyze and compare the projects underlying such bonds. For now, the market remains dominated by multilateral institutions, particularly the World Bank (WB), which has issued close to $8.5 billion in green bonds since 2008, following the launch of its "strategic framework for development and climate change,"[36] and the European Investment Bank (EIB), which has floated "Climate Awareness Bonds." The Asian Development Bank (ADB), the

36   See "About World Bank Green Bonds," treasury.worldbank.org/cmd/htm/WorldBankGreenBonds.html, accessed July 30, 2015.

African Development Bank (AfDB), and the International Monetary Fund (IMF) are also active participants. Such institutions generally issue such bonds to finance renewable or energy-saving projects in developing countries.

Although the themes of climate change and green energy continue to be the focus of these bonds, the past few years have nonetheless witnessed several investment vehicles with social objectives, particularly in the area of public health. The most striking example is that of what are called *Vaccine Bonds*, issued by the International Finance Facility for Immunisation (IFFIm), which now has more than US$4.5 billion of assets under management.

All the instruments described above are guaranteed by their multilateral issuers, and thus enjoy excellent ratings, generally garnering AAA status from ratings agencies. But these issuing institutions do not distinguish, in their accounting, resources derived from green bonds and those from more traditional issues. It is thus impossible to be certain that the new financing is indeed being allocated to "green" projects.

Only a little behind the multilateral institutions, sub-national collectivities (regions, municipalities) in developed countries have recently begun to follow suit. In 2012, France's Île-de-France region undertook a €350 million issuance to finance power projects, energy-efficient social housing, and initiatives to support the social and solidarity economy. Oversubscribed by close to 100%, the success of the bond allowed the region to borrow at an extremely competitive rate of 3.625%. A few years earlier, the Nord-Pas-de-Calais was the first French region to issue a bond specifically dedicated to financing rail transportation infrastructure.

In the United States, several mechanisms have been established in the last few years. Some of these have been spearheaded by local governments, such as New York City, which issued US$339 million worth of "Green Apple Bonds" in 2012, while, in 2013, $100 million in green bonds were floated by the state of Massachusetts. Other initiatives exist at the federal level, as, for instance, a law permitting local authorities to issue "Qualified Energy Conservation Bonds" (QECBs), which are bonds the proceeds of which are exclusively earmarked for energy efficiency or renewable power production projects and offer fiscal advantages for investors.

Yet the most interesting developments are in the corporate world. At the end of 2013, EDF (France's electrical power utility) was the first French company to issue this type of instrument in euros. The success was staggering. The electric company had originally planned to raise €1 billion, but bumped this up to €1.4 billion in the end, which still left the bond twice oversubscribed, as demand amounted to €2.8 billion. In February of 2014, the French real estate company Unibail-Rodamco issued €750 million of a ten-year bond associated with environmental and social constraints—in a matter of hours, the order book totaled €2.5 billion. In the United States, MidAmerican Energy, part of Warren Buffet's Berkshire Hathaway, borrowed US$1 billion to finance solar energy projects. Bank of America led the charge for banking sector issuance of green bonds with a US$500 million issuance in 2013. With these new instruments, corporations accede to sources of financing that are both effective and attractive.

One might think that in order to compensate for the innovative character of these issues, investors might demand slightly higher returns as a sort of risk premium; however, this does not appear to be the case.[37] But the question remains: why does a company like EDF decide to raise capital using an instrument that involves additional constraints? These include increased reporting costs and audits, a heavier burden of disclosure to investors during the launch phase, and other sources of bother. The fact is that traditional bank lending has become more restricted, leaving companies to seek alternative sources of financing. This includes reaching out to different profiles, such as more "responsible" investors. The press releases that accompany corporate green bond issuance never fail to report the percentage of the issue bought by SRI investors.[38]

Monitoring, incentives, and labels

For savers, environmental and social bonds are primarily innovative ways that allow them to direct where their money goes. Novethic's research rightfully highlights the fact that green bonds constitute a "new avenue of progress for responsible investment, based on the final object of the investment itself rather than the ESG quality of the issuer.[39] These products also attract traditional investors looking to integrate ESG criteria and know what projects they will be financing, particularly signatories of the Principles for Responsible Investing (PRI).

---

37 The EDF's "green" bond has a coupon of 2.25%, which is very close to what an EDF traditional issue pays.
38 In the research report *Les obligations environnementales et sociales: un instrument financier prometteur*, published in November 2013, Novethic indicates that 84% of green bonds issued by the African Development Bank (AfDB) were subscribed by "investors with an SRI focus."
39 *Ibid.*

According to a survey conducted by Novethic,[40] 13% of institutional investors have already subscribed to such instruments, or expect to in the immediate future. The Swiss insurance company Zurich has announced that it wishes to become a major green bond player in order to improve the market's liquidity, prompt the participation of other investors, and encourage new issuers. Investments by certain American pension funds, such as CalSTRS and TIAA-CREF, or by asset management companies like Calvert (via the Calvert Green Bond Fund) in the United States, or Mirova in France, are also worth noting. Personal investors remain largely at arm's length from this market, except in Japan, where "Uridashi Climate Bonds" issued by the World Bank or Bank of Norway in certain currencies, particularly dollars, have met with remarkable success.

Obviously, for these institutional investors it is out of the question to sacrifice returns or accept a higher level of risk in exchange for environmental or social benefits. Or, to put it differently, there is no arbitrage between performance and impact. On the other hand, there is a demand for transparency and credible monitoring of environmental and social commitments. Novethic especially insists that the development of green bonds must go hand in hand with "attentive oversight of the projects financed and their impact, in order to avoid the pitfall of greenwashing."[41] Naturally, it is preferable for such bonds to finance new projects, rather than raising money in the sole aim of refinancing existing infrastructure.

---

40   Novethic, *Stratégie ESG des institutionnels: De la théorie à la pratique* (ESG Strategy of Institutional Investors: From Theory to Practice), December 2013.

41   *Ibid.*

Funds raised by the EDF bonds mentioned above were allocated to three projects within the EDF subsidiary Énergies Nouvelles: an onshore wind farm in the South of France, near Perpignan, a solar power plant in California, and another wind project in Canada. The allocations were clearly specified in the bond's termsheet. EDF had, in fact, asked the ratings agency, Vigeo, to approve the eligibility of these projects beforehand, and commissioned the accounting firm of Deloitte to verify *ex post* that funds were employed in accordance with the initial commitments. Vigeo was also called upon for the municipal bond issuances in Nord-Pas-de-Calais and Île-de-France to assess the ESG quality of issuers and appropriateness of projects selected with respect to the bond's theme.

The verification mechanisms in place, however, remain overly vague and lacking in precision. As concerns the issues mentioned above, a possible confusion arises between the two types of rating—the ESG quality of an issuer is no guarantee of a positive environmental or social outcome. Lastly, such ratings are not audits that verify results *ex post*. In North America, certification of results seems to be becoming routine. This can take the form of verification undertaken by an external auditor, like Deloitte in the case of the EDF's green bond, or a label. The AfDB has asked the Center for International Climate and Environmental Research Oslo (CICERO), an independent entity based in Norway, to assess the green bonds it issues. In the long term, the advantage of these bonds resides precisely in their transparency as to the use of funds. It is to be hoped that, well beyond the confines of green bonds themselves, the bond market as a whole will benefit from this trend toward greater transparency regarding resource allocation.

The Climate Bond Initiative provides an extremely broad definition for the notion of green bonds. While, strictly speaking, the market attained less than US$20 billion at the end of 2013, the CBI counted some US$346 billion at March 1, 2013. The reason for this discrepancy is quite simple: in addition to bonds self-identified as green, the CBI counts issuances by companies that operate primarily to limit GHG emissions. This includes all companies in the renewable energy sector, but also all public transportation projects based on clean energy. It is easy to see how such a broad definition can lead to a dilution of the original message.

This is what makes labels so imperative. In December 2010, the CBI thus launched the "Climate Bond Standards,"[42] a tool for evaluating the environmental quality of projects financed by green bonds. To date, no issue has been certified. More recently, several investment banks, including Citi, JP Morgan, BNP Paribas and Crédit Agricole, published a document supported by Ceres[43] providing a detailed description of the *Green Bond Principles*. These principles, which the banks suggest issuers adopt on a voluntary basis, contain a list of domains eligible for financing, and specific requirements in terms of project selection process as well as transparency and reporting. While these initiatives are certainly steps in the right direction, it is impossible that the definition of adequate labels emerge exclusively through a self-regulation process decided on by issuers and investment banks. Two crucial actors are missing from the process as it stands: public authorities and investors. Eligible investments

---

42   See the CBI website: www.climatebonds.net/standards.
43   Ceres (Coalition for Environmentally Responsible Economies) aims to support and encourage a sustainable world economy that respects the environment. Among other activities, the organization performs audits, and issues reports on the sustainable economy.

must correspond to overarching public objectives in the area of social and environmental policy, and be recognized as such. Investors, for their part, need not only to massively subscribe to these new instruments, but also be intransigent as to the quality of green bonds, by insisting on evidence of projects' environmental benefits. Only a coordinated approach that incorporates policy objectives that are democratically defined, clear public incentives, and a well-organized market for green bonds can make it possible to upscale the concept.

A characteristic example of the distribution of roles between public and private sectors is the "Project Bond Initiative" (PBI) established by the EIB as part of its "Europe 2020" strategy.[44] Created in the wake of the Great Financial Crisis (GFC) of 2008, the PBI was designed to rekindle investor appetite for infrastructure projects and long-term debt. Basically, it is a credit enhancement mechanism, based on the observation that most projects lack the intrinsic capacity to issue bonds that are sufficiently "safe," or garner an agency rating of sufficient quality to make them attractive. Thus, such bonds fail to find investors, since the likeliest candidates for such long-term debt are often constrained as to the quality of the debt they purchase, and in general limited to "investment grade" issues. Even though the importance accorded agency ratings is the subject of much debate, the limitations remain a reality. Thus, the EIB intervenes by acquiring a portion of the debt, known as the "mezzanine tranche." This means it will be compensated last, after all other investors. If a problem arises or payment is late, the EIB will be the first to lose. This mechanism stabilizes the balance of the debt to finance

---

44 Coordinated strategy for economic policy within the European Union adopted by members in 2010; the plan covers a horizon of ten years, hence its name.

the project, generally as bonds issued with a superior credit rating, making them more attractive to institutional investors. The program is an ambitious one—€1.2 billion worth of eligible projects were identified as of the end of 2013.

Two operations were implemented in 2013: the financing of Greater Gabbard, an offshore wind farm of 500 MW along the coast of Suffolk, England, and refinancing of the submarine natural gas storage project known as "Castor," in Spain. A third transaction took place in France, in the telecommunications industry.[45] Several more project bonds were issued in 2014 as the pilot phase of the program continued. These included a first issue for Germany, to fund an extension of the A7 speedway, and another road transport project, this time in Belgium.[46] While 2014 saw a number of road transport projects funded, the first issuance of 2015 supported an important piece of infrastructure for the integration of renewable energy: a GBP51 million bond supporting a transmission link (grid hookup) for the world's second largest wind farm, located off the coast of Wales.[47] Nonetheless, it is to be regretted that the projects benefitting from this public initiative are not more clearly directed toward sustainable development. Bond issuances associated with the PBI have been highly successful on the market, thanks

---

45　This involved the refinancing of Axione Infrastructures in July 2014; see press release on corporate website: www.axione.fr/lancement-du-premier-project-bond-francais-et-europeen-dans-le-domaine-du-thd, accessed November 19, 2015.

46　See "The pilot phase of the Europe 2020 Project Bond Initiative," ec.europa.eu/economy_finance/financial_operations/investment/europe_2020/index_en.htm, accessed August 3, 2015.

47　See European Investment Bank, "GBP 51m EIB backing for Gwynt y Mor offshore transmission link," February 13, 2015; www.eib.org/infocentre/press/releases/all/2015/2015-030-gbp-51m-eib-backing-for-gwynt-y-mor-offshore-transmission-link.htm, accessed August 3, 2015.

to several key features: a strategic vision ("Europe 2020"), effective public incentives (PBI), and investor mobilization via products floated on the market. Speaking more generally, the mechanism underlying the PBI, namely the use of public funds to create a lever effect and mobilize private funding, is a keystone of the European Commission's Juncker Plan.[48]

Inventing new models

Building a positive economy also means departing from the traditional frameworks and well-trodden roads of financial capitalism to redefine the function and status of the corporation and encourage behavior consistent with rational altruism. It involves trying out new ways of doing business along with new economic, social, and industrial models that are more collaborative and concerned with the public good. This too requires that finance be innovative to intelligently direct savings. What are these new models? And why are financial mechanisms so essential to their emergence and viability?

Innovating our way through the ecological transition

The ecological and energy transition cannot be reduced to a mere change in how we obtain our electrical energy or to the development of renewable energy sources. The American

---

48   "The new European Fund for Strategic Investments will act as a multiplier. Every public euro mobilised in the Fund will generate about €15 of investment that would not have happened otherwise," according to Vice-president of the European Commission, Jyrki Katainen. Full text available at europa.eu/rapid/press-release_IP-14-2128_en.htm, accessed August 4, 2015.

futurist Jeremy Rifkin probably best explained why the passage from fossil fuels to renewable energy contributes to a profound revolution in how the economy operates. The "Third Industrial Revolution," which he believes imminent, will transform the ultra-concentrated mode of production we have lived with for over a century in a decentralized economy of networks, where the production, not only of energy but of widespread consumer goods, will become local, where the central issue will no longer be how to produce and distribute massively but how to connect, exchange, and collaborate. Strangely, Rifkin hardly mentions finance. In his view, the transition is industrial and behavioral, philosophical at times perhaps, but almost never financial. And yet the transitional phase that is to take us there necessarily involves very hefty investments. It also requires that we master new, unfamiliar technologies and models that will, *a priori,* only provide returns in the long term. Here again, public incentives and private investment must complement each other. The most obvious example of public enhancement of possible private financing lies in renewable energies. The participation of public funds has taken a number of forms according to the country one looks at. In some cases it involves a subsidy to boost the buyback price of electricity so produced, as in France, Spain, and Germany.[49] Other countries, such as the United Kingdom, Denmark, Sweden, or Belgium, issue "green certificates" granting a sort of bonus to renewable energy producers. These green certificates are negotiable instruments (they can be bought and sold), and thus encourage competition within the market. Fixed buyback prices for electricity have accelerated the development of industries related to renewable energy, but carry a significant

---

49 In France, the ERDF purchases, at a rate fixed by the government, electricity individuals produce using, for instance, photovoltaic solar panels.

political risk in the medium term, when the rates come due for renegotiation. But, before the guaranteed buyback rate was implemented in France, the country's renewable energy industry was supported by an innovative financial mechanism: the agency responsible for environmental protection and energy matters, Ademe (*Agence de l'environment et de la maîtrise de l'énergie*), put money into an investment fund stipulating that it would forfeit part of its capital if private investors did not receive the required rate of return.[50] This safety net made it possible to attract a large number of investors and finance quite a lot of projects: wind farms, biodiesel production units, hydroelectric plants, and so on. Where renewable energy is concerned, incentives need to evolve alongside new technologies. Thanks to falling installation costs for solar and wind power, these energy sources are producing better returns, bringing them closer and closer to what is called "grid parity." When grid parity is achieved, public subsidies in their current form will no longer be necessary. However, investors that finance renewable energies have come to take such guaranteed pricing for granted. Soon, those who finance such projects will once again be exposed to the risks associated with fluctuations in the price of electricity. The paradox is that investors may turn against renewables just as their profitability becomes a demonstrated fact. Other mechanisms will be needed to relay those that governments phase out.

As far as thermal renovation of buildings is concerned, the lack of immediate advantages severely hobbles the development of large-scale projects. Analyses show that insulation is the primary "reservoir" of GHG emissions reduction in Western

---

50   Fideme: *Fonds d'investissement de l'environnement et de la maîtrise de l'énergie* (Investment Fund for the Environment and Energy Control).

countries. The buildings sector is the largest overall energy consumer, with close to 40% of consumption and 36% of GHG emissions. Naturally, this makes it a priority objective for public authorities. However, financing energy efficiency projects, whether in residential or industrial constructions, remains a complex matter which combines purely financial problems (solvency of households in the case of residential buildings, distribution of savings between owners and renters, etc.) with technical issues (measurement and monitoring over time of energy savings made possible by renovations), to say nothing of the behavioral and cultural problems involved.[51]

Most of the European Union's 28 member states have established aid programs to encourage improvements in the energy performance of buildings. These measures can be roughly divided into two categories:

- Traditional financial mechanisms that have been deployed since the oil crises of the 1970s. These consist primarily of subsidies, loans, and tax credits. The German example is among the most often cited; the keystone of this energy-saving renovation policy is the extremely low-interest loans offered by the government-owned KfW Development Bank to housing owners.

- Innovative instruments that implicate private investors, particularly Energy Performance Contracts (EPCs) and white certificates (the latter are also called Energy Savings Certificates [ESC], Energy Efficiency Credits [EEC], or white tags). EPCs are contracts between building

---

51   See also a report published by the Buildings Performance Institute Europe (BPIE): *Stimuler la rénovation des bâtiments: un aperçu des bonnes pratiques*; bpie.eu/uploads/lib/document/attachment/28/BPIE_benchmark_EU_obligations_de_r_novation_Nov13.pdf, accessed August 7, 2015

managers and final consumers (municipalities, private leaseholders). Energy Efficiency Credits are designed to encourage households and businesses to save energy by selling their unused credits to industrial players that are failing to meet their regulated limits. These instruments are important because they serve to pull in private capital.

So, how are we to finance the thermal renovation of public buildings over the next ten years? One of the most groundbreaking proposals was prepared by the NGO "Shift Project," and consists of the creation of a corporation for financing the energy transition, which would combine state guarantees with a massive campaign for private funding. This project is one of several on a list likely to be included in the European Commission's stimulus package, known as the Juncker Plan.

It is worth mentioning in passing that the champions of these various projects are all seasoned finance professionals, and that their expertise is one of the keys to creating a balanced equation.

Box 1: The case for a circular economy

In his extended essay *On the Paper Trail*,[52] French novelist Erik Orsenna dispenses philosophical and economic lessons that take the form of an ode to cycles, to the eternal return, the restorative fountain of youth, and infinite recycling of matter. As he explores the highways and byways of paper production, the author urges us to imagine the world differently: "My mind embraced the shape of Nature, where cycles are the

---

52   Erik Orsenna, *Sur la route du papier: Petit précis de mondialisation III* (Paris: Éditions Stock, 2012).

rule, not lines. Responsible growth does not involve striding forward, but a spiral that advances by reusing its waste."

The circular economy grew out of this desire to alter human activity. The economic model we currently adhere to is linear—we extract natural resources, in many cases non-renewable, we transform or consume these resources, and we produce garbage, which, in the best of cases, is recycled, but more often stocked or released into nature. The circular economy proposes to reverse our priorities and shift our attention "from waste management to resource management," to cite the formulation of French deputy François-Michel Lambert, president of the Institute of Circular Economy.[53]

The goal of this project is to bring about a radical change in our prevailing modes of production and consumption. This involves giving precedence to eco-design by taking into account products' end-of-life phase and anticipating the recycling of materials used, encouraging repair and repurposing, and developing ecological industry, in particular by situating production as close as possible to where recyclable products are concentrated—cities will soon be the world's largest producers of raw materials. We must privilege use over acquisition (service economy)[54] and combat programmed obsolescence. The preconditions for this transformation to succeed are at once technological, industrial, psychological, and behavioral. However, they are also financial, a component of the equation that is all too often forgotten here as well.

---

53 In French, the *Institut de l'Économie Circulaire*. See www.institut-economie-circulaire.fr.

54 The service economy aims to substitute for ownership the sale of services or integrated solutions that fulfill or expand on all expected functionalities while consuming fewer resources and energy and creating positive social and environmental externalities.

New business models need creative financing mechanisms based on equally non-traditional analyses of their activities. Providing relevant accounting valuation for these companies involves rethinking of financial engineering. By way of example, Desso, a Dutch manufacturer of wall-to-wall carpeting inspired by the Cradle-to-Cradle philosophy,[55] decided to stop selling their product and contract for a service instead. They now install their carpet and guarantee its use for a specific period, after which they lay new carpeting, retrieving the used, which is recycled according to a proprietary industrial process. The system allows Desso to recycle 95% of the used carpeting, meaning that the circular distribution system ensures the bulk of its long-term need for raw materials. This, in turn, contributes to the company's financial stability. Yet the company experienced difficulty in obtaining financing. Quite simply, the valuation of inventory distributed in a variety of locations rather than a storage facility was, according to bankers, impossible! For this type of economic model to take root effectively, real innovation in the area of accounting and finance are clearly necessary.

Innovating through impact investing

That finance should participate in the energy transition seems fairly logical all around. After all, it constitutes a much-needed return to financing the real economy through a combination of public and private money. The situation is a great deal less clear when it comes to funding social projects such as programs to combat poverty or exclusion, or certain socially useful types of infrastructure. Here we touch on domains traditionally

55   See   www.desso.com/c2c-corporate-responsibility/cradle-to-cradle, accessed November 9, 2015.

dominated by the public sector and non-profit organizations. While this is particularly true in France, it holds for the majority of Western democracies. The intrusion of private-sector financing in this area can appear surprising, even alarming. A deep-seated suspicion tells us that there is an irremediable incompatibility between positive social objectives and the venal cynicism that rules the financial world.

Nonetheless, many social programs today are confronted by the harsh reality of shrinking public budgets. Is it possible to imagine financial innovations that reconcile the returns required by long-term savings with the resolution of social problems? The concept of a "social return" associated with an investment gives rise to financing mechanisms that lie at the crossroads of public, private, and associative action, combining the contributions of each sector. Such instruments are broadly known as "impact investing," a term first used in 2007 by the Rockefeller Foundation.

According to a 2009 study by the Monitor Institute, impact investing could become a $500 billion industry within a few years.[56] The category currently comprises a wide variety of investments, primarily in areas such as social inclusion, sustainable development, social housing, and development aid projects in poor countries, including microfinance initiatives.[57] So, are

---

56   Jessica Freireich and Katherine Fulton, *Investing for Social and Environmental Impact* (Boston: The Monitor Institute, 2009). Available at www.monitorinstitute.com/downloads/what-we-think/impact-investing/ Impact_Investing.pdf, accessed August 8, 2015.

57   It is worth noting that social needs are difficult to distinguish from other types discussed in this volume. Access to energy is as much a social question as it is an environmental issue, for instance, and education intersects with concerns over social access to knowledge and various questions of digital content.

social and solidarity investors necessarily missionaries? It is true that the underlying projects funded by these mechanisms usually exhibit aspects of a crusade. Not only are they often pushing against tremendous forces, they usually seem, to outsiders at least, merely a drop in the ocean. Scaling-up is thus a hugely important issue. How can we channel the sums that get invested and the projects supported into the mainstream economy, so that they have a place at the heart of the system rather than its periphery?

As a factor in both encouraging growth and social cohesion, the social and solidarity economy is on the European agenda. Launched in 2011 by Michel Barnier, who was at that time the European Commissioner in charge of the European single market and services, the Social Business Initiative (SBI) is specifically targeted at social enterprise: that is, businesses pursuing objectives that contribute to the general good (social, societal, or environmental) rather than a strict profit maximization. The initiative has a financing component based on the creation of European Social Entrepreneurship Funds (EuSEF), which now enjoy their own European label.

Generally speaking, public authorities have all pronounced themselves in favor of developing impact investing. Following the G8 meeting in 2013, a working group presided over by Sir Ronald Cohen was convened in order to coordinate the development of financial innovations designed to address social problems. It is clear that governments play a key role in the expansion of impact investment via their capacity to provided needed incentives. Their actions can be broken down into three types:

- Using public funds to increase the numbers of private actors involved by making such investments more attractive or reducing their risk levels. The British initiative mentioned earlier, Big Society Capital, falls into this category, as do funds like those created under the European Investment Fund (EIF) or by Bpifrance in France.

- Facilitating and stabilizing social investments by providing logistical platforms or technical infrastructure that ensure secure transactions.

- Creating and promoting quality labels that uphold stringent criteria.

Through these mechanisms, private money can finance social programs that previously relied solely on government funds. Social Impact Bonds (SIBs) offer another approach. In contrast with the social and environmental issues discussed earlier, SIBs are not, properly speaking, bond issues. The mechanism is much more akin to that of a PPP, insofar as a municipality delegates the implementation of a social program to a private-sector agent, with private investors providing the funding needed. SBIs have been used, notably to finance programs for rehabilitation and anti-recidivism programs, social housing and services for the homeless using private money. The principle of these instruments is that investors are reimbursed only if the program successfully meets its stated objectives. For instance, the first British SBI was aimed at reducing the rate of recidivism at Peterborough Prison by 7.5%. Below that threshold, investors risked losing a portion of their invested capital. Contracts such as these help align the interests of public authorities, a project's management, and investors. Municipalities finance only projects that can demonstrate results, the promoters get their funding, and investors achieve an attractive return if the project meets its goals. In the medium term, this is one way to select the most effective social practices in certain domains.

Social impact bonds were developed in the UK, initially thanks to a program instituted by the Ministry of Justice and a UK-based foundation known as Social Finance; however, other countries have since climbed aboard. The City of New York, for instance, employed an instrument of this kind to finance an education and training program for prisoners at its Riker's Island prison facility. This is not to say that SIBs are exempt from criticism. On a political level, some fear that they encourage authorities to ignore their responsibilities in areas that traditionally devolve to the government. On a moral level, concerns have been voiced as to whether investors may legitimately extract substantial remuneration from social projects with significant human impact. We disagree with this view. As with green bonds, and Responsible Investment broadly speaking, the commitment of investors strikes us as the key to successful implementation of these new tools, assuming, of course, that these private actors are long-term-focused and demanding as to the quality and existence of the social impacts involved.

Box 2: The case for microfinance

Ever since the success of the Grameen Bank and the Nobel Prize awarded to its founder Muhammad Yunus, microfinance has been a recognized and respected activity. Institutions dedicated to this type of financing have multiplied in India, as well as Latin America and Africa. The model has experienced its share of difficulties, including the bankruptcy and over indebtedness of certain institutions, and debates over its purview and definition. Nonetheless, microfinance did irrefutably demonstrate the idea that a financial innovation could be structured around a social priority: reducing poverty, which gave rise to what we know as "inclusive finance."

Financing the poorest members of our societies and meeting the needs of the "bottom of the pyramid" requires that we move beyond traditional market mechanisms. It also calls for a different way of mobilizing savings, one that is more local and/or more direct. By and large, the microfinance model does not rely on government subsidies: its primary source of financing consists of the savings deposited by clients. More generally, creating a direct conduit between micro-lenders and micro-borrowers is also an essential principle distinguishing participative funding platforms, also known as "crowdfunding," that are taking shape in the United States and Europe.

5

Conclusion

The turmoil that afflicted the market in 2007 and 2008 provoked an unprecedented wave of regulation. In Europe especially, where the banking system provides 70% of corporate financing, ensuring the stability of banks seemed an essential precondition for any return to growth. "Never again will taxpayers be forced to bail out a bank,"[1] promised politicians of all stripes. Measures were immediately taken: increased solvency

---

1   Variations on this phrase were pronounced by Barak Obama in 2010 (see Jesse Lee, "President Obama: 'Never again will the American taxpayer be held hostage by a bank that is "too big to fail"'," January 21, 2010; https://www.whitehouse.gov/blog/2010/01/21/president-obama-never-again-will-american-taxpayer-be-held-hostage-a-bank-too-big-fa) and Mark Carney, Governor of the Bank of England (see J. Titcomb, "Mark Carney: No more bank bail-outs" *Telegraph,* November 10, 2014; www.telegraph.co.uk/finance/newsbysector/banksandfinance/11220192/Mark-Carney-No-more-bank-bail-outs.html). Angela Merkel proposed similar measures; see Tony Czuczka and Nicholas Comfort, "Let banks fail to save taxpayers: Merkel," *Financial Post,* April 15, 2013; business.financialpost.com/news/economy/let-banks-fail-to-save-taxpayers-merkel, accessed November 19, 2015.

ratios, new liquidity requirements, a new category of "Systemi-
cally Important Financial Institutions" (known as SIFIs, these
are banks considered "too big to fail"), a European mechanism
for resolving banking crises, a battery of "stress tests," bank
audits and new rules for reporting, and, finally, European banking union under the supervision of the ECB.

Such regulatory and prudential topics are not the focus of this
book. While the stability of banks should by no means be considered irrelevant, safe banking is more of a prerequisite: a necessary, but not a sufficient condition. Public authorities have
been behaving schizophrenically: on the one hand demanding
that the financial system support growth, while simultaneously
imposing all sorts of constraints that severely hamper its ability
to do this. Making sustainable growth a reality means breaking
the cycle of crisis and sanctions to forge a new identity for the
financial world. Finance needs to be seen, and to behave, as a
cog, a belt, a mechanism. In short, it must become a tool in the
service of actual goals. This is where the question of what we do
with long-term savings becomes an issue of central importance.
We need to find a way to direct this funding toward the most
positive sectors, those making useful contributions. Our economies have no paucity of savings—the Euro Zone exhibits a stable savings rate that currently hovers around 14%, comparable
to what it was before the financial crisis. The amount of capital
pooled in pension funds and insurance schemes is enormous.
Yet it remains difficult to finance innovation, small and medium-
sized businesses, or the infrastructure needed by the green economy. However, it is increasingly clear that savings need to be
reallocated to the long term, and that private capital has to be
channeled into the emergence of a carbon-free world that is
socially stable and inclusive.

Is it possible for finance and those associated with it to regain a certain amount of trust? Evidence from the myriad initiatives that have sprung up in the areas of financing the energy transition, responsible investing and impact investing, among others, demonstrates that there is a way this can happen. What conditions need to be met if we are to amplify these initiatives, overcome inertia, and move responsible investing from the periphery to the center of our markets?

Definitions

Defining what responsible savings should look like requires that we clearly picture the world we wish to create and bring the power of democratic governance to bear on market forces. Defining and establishing the rules of the game is overwhelmingly a task for public authorities. Describing precisely what constitutes a sustainable Public–Private Partnership, a positive infrastructure project, a Responsible Investment fund or a "green" bond, for instance, all fall under this category.

How should we define responsible investing?

It is high time that we ceased setting up an opposition between Responsible Investment and "traditional" saving. There is no reason to choose between social and environmental and performance on the one hand and financial returns on the other. Defining responsible investing needs to focus on ends rather than means and bring to the fore its goals and relationship to sustainable development rather than being based entirely on how asset management companies go about obtaining such results, which is to say the integration of ESG (environmental, social, and governance) criteria. The central question needs to be not "how is it done?" but "what does it achieve?"

Here, various stakeholders have different contributions to make: democratic bodies need to define objectives and establish specifications, whereas it falls to the financial actors to come up with practical methods, provide expertise, create labels, and measure impact.

Labels

Choice is integral to the very act of investing. In and of itself, an investment constitutes a selection; it thus behooves us to ask: What company or project do we want to finance? And, conversely, what companies do we wish to stay away from? In an ideal world, the sum of all individual decisions, based as they are on a variety of circumstantial criteria—savings objectives, investment horizon, personal and financial situation, greater or lesser appetite for risk, etc.—would advance the general good. However, this natural arrangement does not suffice on its own. It is therefore essential that we understand what motivates the choices of savers. What are they looking for? Having done this, it becomes possible to imagine several levers that could be used to orient savings.

- The first of these undoubtedly involves greater transparency and improved information for savers. Financial instruments are frequently opaque and overly complex, with the result that distributors hold all the cards. Informing people so they can understand products, in particular by ensuring transparency as to factors such as their objectives, the investments involved, their performance, fees, etc., is certainly a good place to start.

- It is next important to make responsible saving as attractive as possible, via appropriate regulation and fiscal policies.

- Lastly, it is crucial to demonstrate how individual savers are linked to the general well-being. No investor wants his or her savings to contribute to making life more difficult in the future, to say nothing of impossible; however, people don't automatically understand how their choices can influence the world they live in.

No major change can take place without popular support, the population in question here being household savers. For this reason, the issue needs to be thought of within the wider context of a movement for a positive economy. This involves an educational component, to prove to individuals that their savings have a determining effect, just like the products and services they consume do. By definition, savings are a shift of consumption from the present to the future—they transport money through time. All the more natural, one would think, to take into account the impact of these present choices on the generations to come.

Creating labels that acknowledge and uphold the quality of responsible savings vehicles or positive finance would provide a mechanism for directly and efficiently relating public goals and private decisions. Delivered by recognized organizations granted the means to communicate and increase awareness and associated with public incentives, these labels would serve two distinct purposes:

- Provide individual investors with transparent information regarding investment vehicles;

- Effectively incentivize savings allocation—enhancing the attractiveness of responsible instruments thanks to measures by public authorities: namely, regulation and taxation.

Quality labels are extremely important for consumers in a wide range of industries. The obvious examples, such as "Organic" and "Fair Trade" spring to mind, but there are many others, in the area of forestry, paper production, for instance, or electric vehicles, to say nothing of the energy consumption of household appliances. Where savings are concerned, however, financial products are more likely to be identified in terms of the applicable fiscal or regulatory statutes—equity savings plan, whole or term life insurance policies, etc.—than by the type of projects or companies they actually finance. As a result, responsible savings are hard to identify and, predictably, Responsible Investment is relatively unknown. According to a survey conducted in France by the FIR (*Forum pour l'Investissement Responsible*, or Responsible Investment Forum), 70% of those polled claimed never to have heard of "SRI" asset management. Even among the remaining 30%, only a minority could define the term.

There are currently several labels in Europe that identify responsible investment vehicles.

- The "Novethic" label, launched in 2009, is conferred on French and European funds by the eponymous subsidiary of the Caisse des Dépôts et Consignations. Novethic awarded its SRI label to about a hundred products, using a proprietary methodology that is stringent and based on regular exchanges with sector professionals that sit on its technical advisory board. In 2013, Novethic also created a "Green Label" to identify funds specifically dedicated to environmental themes.

- The German Sustainable Investment Forum (FNG: *Forum Nachhaltige Geldanlagen*) began work in 2014 on a project to label German SRI funds. After carefully establishing the specifications, the FNG put out a call for bids to select an organization to be responsible for analyzing funds and awarding the label. Novethic was the candidate retained for this task, an encouraging step toward the possibility of a European-wide label in the future.

- The Luxemburg association LuxFLAG, which is supported by the Grand Duchy, is worth noting for its three labels devoted to microfinance, investment funds for a positive environment, and, more recently, to ESG funds. Today, some 40 funds have received these labels.

- A number of other labels exist in Europe. In France, the union label CIES is reserved for employee savings funds and the Finansol label for solidarity funds; in Belgium and Austria, professional associations have verification procedures for certain characteristics of SRI funds.

- Lastly, Eurosif decided not to establish a label as such, and is content to apply its logo to funds that meet its transparency requirements.

Asset management professionals have also taken steps to label certain of their offerings in order to "certify" the quality of their services. In 2010, AXA Investment Managers, for example, elected to undergo the certification of their SRI investment process by an external auditor (Deloitte), an arrangement they have renewed each year since. In 2013, Amundi had its SRI process certified by AFNOR, the organization that represents ISO norms in France.

Enhanced reporting requirements applicable to members of the PRI could also, as they emerge, give rise to a genuine certification process that establishes ESG integration criteria on a global scale.

Incentives

What purpose is served by labeling products that contribute to positive finance? Labels help to create an ecosystem that promotes Corporate Social Responsibility, long-term investment in infrastructure, and the use of savings to improve the lives of vulnerable populations. The foundation of such an ecosystem is a partnership between public and private enterprise that clearly sets out the roles of each, and defines what ought to be decided democratically and what can be handled by market mechanisms.

This all comes down to the following:

- Encouraging distributors to offer their clients responsible savings vehicles: every whole life insurance policy and every fund type proposed by retail banks ought to have at least one SRI fund;

- Reserving fiscal incentives for funds that meet quality label standards: for instance, by exempting them from the future—though currently hypothetical—tax on financial transactions (TFT) introduced by the European Union;

- Requiring institutional investors to annually disclose the percentage of assets held in SRI labeled funds. This would be not unlike the requirement France (the first country to take this step) has implemented as of May 2015: that all institutional investors calculate and publish the carbon footprint of their portfolios;

- Making investments in responsible assets more attractive by adjusting the applicable rules used to calculate prudential ratios for banks and insurers.

Labels are by no means a silver bullet. However, this is where change can and must take place: at the crossroads where public policy, the behavior of the many households that consume and save, and initiatives by private actors in the world of finance meet.

What we need in order to make the energy transition a reality is "positive" finance. Positive Finance acknowledges that it needs to rethink its models, and is founded on the intelligent use of public incentives, while eschewing overreliance on windfall effects. Positive Finance incorporates environmental and social dimensions in the investment process; it recognizes and supports technological innovation. This is a challenge we can meet. Finance is only a tool, not an end in itself; it is high time this instrument was used in the service of higher goals: namely, a positive economy.

Glossary

Anthropocene. Proposed in 2002 by Paul Crutzen, recipient of the Nobel Prize in Chemistry, this term is employed to designate the current geological era as having begun with the Industrial Revolution. The primary characteristic of this new era is seen to be the pervasive influence of human activity on the environmental on a global level (including loss of biodiversity, climate change, etc.).

Benchmark. Often abbreviated as "bench," a benchmark, in finance, is a reference index that serves as a point of comparison for evaluating the performance of asset managers.

Bottom of the pyramid (BOP). This expression, popularized by economist C.K. Prahalad, describes the four and some billion individuals worldwide who live on less than US$2.50 per day. For some economists, this segment of the population, frequently ignored by the financial industry and businesses, potentially represents a significant market, as human needs exist regardless of income. According to these thinkers, a creative and entrepreneurial approach to the poor to offer them suitable products and services has the potential to reduce poverty.

Business as usual. This expression is employed in reference to the prevailing attitude of companies that base their activities on reproducing the status quo. In a "business as usual" scenario, economic agents pay no attention to emerging environmental issues, particularly the need to reduce greenhouse gas emissions.

Climate Awareness Bonds. These securities, created by the European Investment Bank in 2007, serve to finance projects whose ambition is to reduce greenhouse gas emissions—usually in the areas of renewable energy or energy efficiency.

Inclusive finance. Also known as financial inclusion, inclusive finance offers financial services (such as access to a bank account or bank card and recourse to credit or savings) to low-income populations, known as the unbanked or underbanked, often situated in emerging or developing economies. In order to reduce financial exclusion—tantamount to social exclusion—inclusive finance provides consumer information and offers microloans and other products suited to circumstances.

Best-in-class funds. Funds identified as best-in-class which rely on ESG (environmental, social, and governance) criteria select those companies that achieve the best extra-financial ratings within their sector or industry. This approach ensures that fund managers can invest in any sector, regardless of its social or environmental impacts.

European Social Entrepreneurship Fund (ESEF). This is a European-level label established under the Social Business Initiative that identifies fund managers 70% of whose investments are made in unlisted companies that list social priorities in their articles of incorporation. The label facilitates European-wide commercialization for funds it is accorded to.

Green bonds. First launched in the United States, then picked up by the World Bank, "qualified green building and sustainable design project bonds" to name them in full, are what we call "green bonds." They are used to finance infrastructure beneficial to sustainable development and environmental protection, such as wind farms and solar energy parks. One of their distinguishing features is a total disclosure requirement, whereby issuers must compile detailed reports on the projects financed by these instruments and make them available to investors.

Greenwashing. This qualifier describes the media strategy of companies or organizations that attempt to purvey an environmentally responsible image without following through on ecologically sound actions in keeping with their "green talk." For these entities, financial motives trump the individual and collective responsibility to preserve our planet's resources.

Grid parity. This refers to the financial profitability of renewable energy and designates the point at which the cost of producing renewable energy (largely solar or wind power for now) takes place, exclusive of subsidies, at a cost that is less than or equal to that of conventional energy production.

Impact investing. Impact investing is a catchall term which aggregates a variety of investments that aim to provide social returns, meaning projects that combine positive financial yield and specific social and/or environmental returns on investment.

Microfinance, of which microloans are one aspect, designates the spectrum of financial services offered to those individuals excluded from the conventional banking system (the unbanked and underbanked). These services include loans for very small sums ranging from a few euros to a few thousand (microloans), savings vehicles, insurance coverage, etc.

UNEP Finance Initiative (UNEP-FI). The financial initiative of the United Nations Environmental Programme (UNEP) is a Public–Private Partnership between the UNEP and the financial industry. More than 200 public and private organizations, banks, asset management, and insurance companies work hand in hand to promote the concept of sustainable development within financial institutions, particularly by championing the integration of ESG criteria in the analysis of risk. The Principles for Responsible Investment (PRI) grew out of the UNEP-FI.

Public–Private Partnership (PPP). Public–Private Partnerships are long-term financing mechanisms whereby a public authority engages a private firm to provide a public service. These can range from construction projects to the upkeep and management of public utilities. PPPs can make it possible to complete complex projects more quickly and respond dynamically to urgent municipal needs.

Social Impact Bond (SIB). These "pay for success bonds" are debt instruments guaranteed by the state that are essentially wagers on social returns. They solicit private investment to finance projects that are then undertaken by public entities. If the organization fails to meet its social objectives, investors lose their stake. If, however, the project is successful, investors recoup their investment, plus a percentage of the sums economized by the project's implementation.

Primary organizations cited

Association française de la gestion financière (AFG)

This association brings together actors from the world of asset management to address issues of concern to the industry. Members, which are asset management companies, entrepreneurs, or subsidiaries of banks and insurance companies, may be mandated, or be managers of UCITs.

CDC Climat

This subsidiary of the Caisse des Dépôts, created in 2013, is entirely dedicated to the ecological and energy transition. The institution conducts economic research, develops innovative projects, and provides financing to support municipalities and companies in implementing their energy–climate transition strategies.

Cicero

The Center for International Change and Environmental Research is an independent think-tank and research center created by the government of Norway in 1990 in partnership with the University of Oslo. The center conducts research and provides reliable data on impacts related to climate change.

Climate Bonds Initiative (CBI)

The Climate Bonds Initiative is an international organization that lobbies to promote long-term financial debt, and offers solution for investors, NGOs, and governments to shape bond issues that support low-carbon projects. The CBI also issues certifications that identify "responsible climate bonds."

European Investment Bank (EIB)

The European Investment Bank belongs to the 28 members of the European Union. The institution borrows money on the financial markets, which it uses to finance projects that improve infrastructure, energy production, and environmental performance, whether within the EU and neighboring countries, or developing countries.

Finansol

Finansol is a French association whose mission is to promote socially responsible savings vehicles that increase access to employment and housing for struggling populations and to encourage ecologically responsible business practices and entrepreneurship. Since 1997, the organization also issues a label bearing its name.

Forum pour l'investissement responsable (FIR)

Founded in 2001, the Forum pour l'investissement responsable (Responsible Investment Forum) is a French professional body devoted to promoting Socially Responsible Investment. The FIR brings together actors from throughout the SRI value chain: investors, asset management companies, ratings agencies, traders, investment advisors, professional bodies, and unions.

Green Growth Group

The Green Growth Group is a working group comprised of ministers from 13 European countries (Belgium, Denmark, Estonia, Finland, France, Germany, Italy, the Netherlands, Portugal, Slovenia, Spain, Sweden, and the United Kingdom) that share a common outlook on questions related to the environment, energy policy, and climate concerns. Their role is to design and promote an effective and profitable carbon reduction scheme to encourage European growth. In October 2013, the group published *Going for Green Growth,* a document that underscored the need for the European Union to take forceful and immediate regulatory measures to limit carbon consumption in Europe.

Monitor Institute

Based in Boston, Massachusetts, the Monitor Institute, which is a subsidiary of Monitor Deloitte, operates both as a consulting group and a think-tank which seeks to develop new approaches that can help corporations implement strategies for addressing social and environmental problems, notably through the effective use of technologies and partnerships.

Novethic

A subsidiary of the French Caisse des Dépôts, Novethic is a platform dedicated to sustainable development and a center for research and expertise on Corporate Social Responsibility and socially responsible investing. Novethic analyzes broad trends in SRI and published annual statistics for the French market. The organization confers a label, launched in 2009, based on environmental, social, and governance (ESG) factors.

Acronyms and abbreviations

Ademe	*Agence de l'environnement et de la maîtrise de l'énergie* (French Agency for the Environment and Energy Safety)
AFG	*Association française de la gestion financière* (French Association of Asset Management Professionals)
CBI	Climate Bonds Initiative
CSR	Corporate Social Responsibility
EIB	European Investment Bank
ESPC	Energy Savings Performance Contract
Fideme	*Fonds d'investissement de l'environnement et de la maîtrise de l'énergie* (Investment Fund for the Environment and Control of Energy)
FIR	*Forum pour l'investissement responsable* (Responsible Investment Forum)
PEA-PME	*Plan d'épargne en actions de petites et moyennes entreprises* (Savings Plan in the Equity of Small and Medium-Sized Enterprises)

PBI	Project Bond Initiative
PPP	Public–Private Partnership
PRI	Principles for Responsible Investment (also written UN-PRI)
SIB	Social Impact Bond
SRI	Socially Responsible Investing

About the authors

Hervé Guez
Director, Responsible Investment Research, Mirova

Hervé is a Certified International Investment Analyst (CIIA®) who has amassed 12 years of buy- and sell-side experience in both equities and credit. This considerable experience of finance convinced him that the financial markets could better fulfill their role of usefully allocating capital, notably by incorporating more directly the social and environmental issues that loom increasingly large for both public corporations and the public as a whole. He subsequently headed up SRI research at Mirova[1] as Director, a position he has occupied since 2008. The philosophy and methodology he developed are currently employed by the Responsible Investment Research division's 11 analysts to guide the integration of ESG criteria across the whole of Natixis[2] Asset Management, and as a basis for the investment strategies pursued by Mirova's actively managed sustainability-themed conviction funds in the realms of equities, fixed income, and infrastructure. The group furthermore publishes regular in-depth

---

1 Mirova is a wholly owned subsidiary of Natixis Asset Management.
2 Natixis Asset Management is an affiliate of Natixis Global Asset Management, a wholly owned subsidiary of Natixis.

research, both independently and in partnership with the University of Cambridge. Hervé serves on the board of the French SIF (Social Investment Forum), and represents Mirova within the UNEP-Finance Initiative, the PRI (Principles for Responsible Investment), Eurosif (European Sustainable Investment Forum) and the SRI commission of the AFG, as well as sitting on the board of the Green Bond Principles.

Philippe Zaouati
CEO, Mirova

Philippe is the CEO and co-founder of Mirova, a Groupe BPCE asset management company dedicated to Responsible Investment. Mirova currently manages around €5.7 billion across equities, fixed income, infrastructure, and impact investing. Prior to his tenure at Mirova, Philippe was Deputy CEO of Natixis Asset Management. For nearly a decade, Philippe Zaouati has contributed to the development of responsible finance across Europe, in particular through his role in various professional associations and international organizations, including the creation of the Investment Leaders Group (ILG) in partnership with the University of Cambridge, an initiative that brings together top executives from leading asset management companies and institutional investors. He also actively contributes to the Movement for a Positive Economy. His first book on the topic, *Investir "Responsable": en quête de nouvelles valeurs pour la finance* (Lignes de Repères Éditions), came out in 2009. Philippe is a graduate of the ENSAE (École Nationale de la Statistique et de l'Administration Économique) and an accredited member of the Institut des Actuaires Français (French Society of Actuaries). He is a laureate of the French national Concours Général in History and has published two novels to date: *La fumée qui gronde* (arHsens édiTions, 2011) and *Naufrages* (Les Éditions des Rosiers, 2014).

For Product Safety Concerns and Information please contact our EU
representative GPSR@taylorandfrancis.com
Taylor & Francis Verlag GmbH, Kaufingerstraße 24, 80331 München, Germany

www.ingramcontent.com/pod-product-compliance
Ingram Content Group UK Ltd.
Pitfield, Milton Keynes, MK11 3LW, UK
UKHW021025180425
457613UK00021B/1068